WINNIPEG

WITHDRAWN

PUBLIC LIBRARY

D0044735

Penguin
LIVES

Martin Luther

A LIPPER™/ VIKING BOOK

GENERAL EDITOR: JAMES ATLAS

MARTIN MARTY

Martin Luther

A Penguin Life

A LIPPER™/ VIKING BOOK

VIKING
Published by the Penguin Group
Penguin Group (USA) Inc., 375 Hudson Street,
New York, New York 10014, U.S.A.
Penguin Books Ltd, 80 Strand, London WC2R oRL, England
Penguin Books Australia Ltd, 250 Camberwell Road, Camberwell,
Victoria 3124, Australia
Penguin Books Canada Ltd, 10 Alcorn Avenue,
Toronto, Ontario, Canada M4V 3B2
Penguin Books India (P) Ltd, 11 Community Centre, Panchsheel Park,
New Delhi–110 017, India
Penguin Books (N.Z.) Ltd, Cnr Rosedale and Airborne Roads, Albany,
Auckland, New Zealand
Penguin Books (South Africa) (Pty) Ltd, 24 Sturdee Avenue,
Rosebank, Johannesburg 2196, South Africa

Penguin Books Ltd, Registered Offices:
80 Strand, London WC2R oRL, England

First published in 2004 by Viking Penguin,
a member of Penguin Group (USA) Inc.

1   3   5   7   9   10   8   6   4   2

Copyright © Martin Marty, 2004
All rights reserved

Maps by Micah Marty

Grateful acknowledgment is made for permission to reprint an excerpt from
"Luther" from *Collected Poems* by W. H. Auden. Copyright © 1976 by Edward
Mendelson, William Meredith, and Monroe K. Spears, Executors of the Estate of
W. H. Auden. Used by permission of Random House, Inc.

CIP data available
ISBN 0-670-03272-7

This book is printed on acid-free paper. ∞

Printed in the United States of America
Set in Janson Text   Designed by Francesca Belanger

Without limiting the rights under copyright reserved above, no part of this publication may be reproduced, stored in or introduced into a retrieval system, or
transmitted, in any form or by any means (electronic, mechanical, photocopying,
recording, or otherwise), without the prior written permission of both the copyright owner and the above publisher of this book.

The scanning, uploading, and distribution of this book via the Internet or via any
other means without the permission of the publisher is illegal and punishable by
law. Please purchase only authorized electronic editions and do not participate in
or encourage electronic piracy of copyrighted materials. Your support of the author's rights is appreciated.

To Mark U. Edwards Jr.
on whose presidential office wall at St. Olaf College,
where we worked together and where I learned so much,
was posted this from Luther:

God does not save people who are only fictitious sinners.
Be a sinner and sin boldly
but believe and rejoice in Christ even more boldly,
for he is victorious over sin, death,
and the world.

". . . All works, Great Men, Societies are bad.
  The Just shall live by Faith . . ." he cried in dread.

And men and women of the world were glad,
Who'd never cared or trembled in their lives.

                                    W. H. Auden, 1940

Preface

MARTIN LUTHER is the story of Martin Luther, not a history of the Protestant Reformation, though its subject was the most prominent figure in the combined religious and political stirrings of sixteenth-century Europe. While his name appeared near the top in the inevitable rankings of "most influential people" of the millennium past, not until a brief afterword does this book include a measure of his influence, examine his legacy, or visit the twenty-first century.

Curiously, for all the academic and popular attention long given him, at the time of this writing only three or four biographies of Luther are in print in English. Librarians report that few historical figures have received more monographic scholarly attention than he. Such scholarship has informed its author, but this Penguin Life is not and cannot be an extended entry into the debates that it inspires. There are suggestions for further reading in the final pages.

Nor is this the work of either a hanging judge or a flack. The flaws that blighted Luther's reputation, such as in his relation to peasants in 1524–25 or to Jews late in his life, are gross, obvious, and, in the latter case, even revolting. While it is tempting for us contemporary scholars to parade our moral credentials by competing to see who can most extravagantly condemn historical figures such as Luther, in this story wherever denunciation would be in order his words and actions will show him condemning himself without much help from this biographer interfering as a righteous scold.

Conversely, as for possible efforts at biographical public relations on Luther's behalf: For his positive contributions to the development of human liberty, the free expression of conscience, support of music, development of literary style, and his role in reshaping religious life, he needs no advertiser, and readers will not find one here.

This portrait of Martin Luther will not depict a modern person, because he was not one. Those devoted to periodizing in history might call him a late-medieval contributor to the early modern scene. He left tantalizing and often unsubtle clues that credibly evoke deep psychological assessments, and touching on them here will contribute to but cannot begin to exhaust efforts at accounting for some dimensions of his personality.

He makes most sense as a wrestler with God, indeed, as a God-obsessed seeker of certainty and assurance in a time of social trauma and of personal anxiety, beginning with his own. Those who bring passion to what is a universal search for meaning in life may well identify with such a search, though of course by no means all will find Luther's resolution attractive or even accessible, because it appears in a Christian framework. People of other faiths or of no explicit religious commitment may find his specific solutions alien, but they can grasp what he was about by analogy to approaches that they already find familiar from other studies of literature and history or from their own experiences.

This account consistently connects the story of Luther's inner experiences with that of his relations to the external surroundings. Biographers of controversial, spiritually profound figures regularly receive warnings that in a changed world, often described as secular, publics cannot identify with or find relevant inner struggles that reflect remote times and places. Yet moderns who cannot picture receiving direct messages from God, like those Joan of Arc claimed, have little difficulty discerning how her response to such messages changed French and English history and why it is urgent to pay attention to her own accounting. Few people have mystical experiences like those of Bernard of Clairvaux, but awareness of his informs the understanding of his preaching to support crusades. Stories of Francis of Assisi's stigmata, which looked like replications of the wounds of Christ on his body, sound incredible to most of us, but dealing with them is crucial for anyone who would come to terms with his impact on medieval life.

In the present case, perhaps most contemporaries cannot identify with Luther's sense of guilt and dread in the face of an angry God, yet what he made of his struggles is integral to the story of modern Europe—indeed, the modern world. If it is true that fewer people today struggle with guilt before God while more have difficulty facing anomaly and absurdity, finding meaning in life in the face of an apparently indifferent universe, or embracing firm faith of any sort, many of them may find in Luther a classic case of one facing such difficulties, seeking meaning, often doubting, and even falling into despair until he grasped faith, or it grasped him.

As for genre: A century ago historians of theology held a near monopoly among scholars dealing with religious figures like Luther. In his case, during the past half century social historians have impressively chronicled and analyzed the cultural context, though often at the expense of attention to his ideas and beliefs. Today, in a world where personal spiritual quests and global religious conflicts alike are familiar, we can expect that many readers will welcome the kind of cultural history or biography that pays attention both to those theological themes and to their settings in monastery, home, church, university, and empire.

One sometime hears that in a secular and religiously pluralist culture, theological language and ideas may sound arcane and forbidding, and one should play them down. That makes little sense when a biographer deals with the life of a theologian who had an immense bearing on the world around him, since such a figure drew on theological language and ideas. Biographies of, for example, an astronomer, a microbiologist, an athlete, or a politician must invite readers to the complex thought worlds, in turn, of astronomy, microbiology, athletics, and politics. Thanks to his gift for pithy and salty expression and his passion for transgressing linguistic and social boundaries, Martin Luther makes it possible for a biographer with some ease to invite into his world people who might, in the normal course of things, stand outside it. It is the biographer's task to make them feel sufficiently at home in that world that they can make judgments about the story and sufficiently ill at ease in it that the telling can provoke them into fresh thinking.

Observers of the art of biography in recent years have regularly noted that beginning the story of a life with the birth and ending with the death of a subject, an approach dismissed by some in the not too distant past in favor of essays on theory, is coming to find renewed favor. I will begin with Luther's birth and end his story at his death, largely leaving to others the accounts of his posthumous influence and its global consequences.

Contents

Locations of Luther sites on a map
of modern Germany

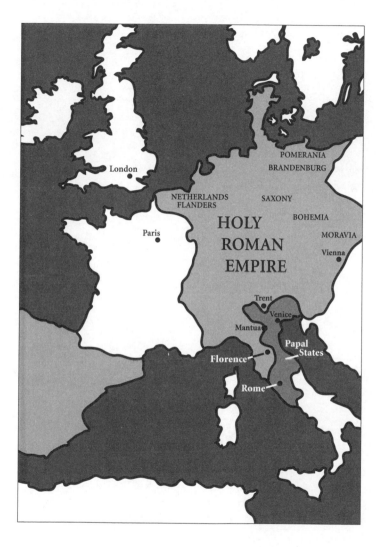

*The Holy Roman Empire
in the time of Luther*

Martin Luther

CHAPTER ONE

The Hunger for Certainty
1483–1519

SHORTLY BEFORE MIDNIGHT one November 10, probably in 1483, in the Saxon town of Eisleben, Margarethe Lindemann Luder gave birth to a son. When he was grown and had made enemies, some of them charged that this "beloved mother" had been a whore and bath attendant. Not at all. She was instead a hardworking woman of trading-class stock and middling means. When he did later write of her, Luther remembered Margarethe as someone who could punish him severely. Parents in her time and place routinely did that. But, he recalled, she had meant heartily well.

His father, Hans Luder or Ludher—later Luther—was a leaseholder of mines and smelters. He was to become respectable enough to serve as one of four citizens who represented others before a town council. This ambitious and occasionally jovial father could likewise be a harsh disciplinarian, but—as Martin also said of him—Hans had meant heartily well.

Eisleben, where the family lived for only a few months after the child's birth, straddled the edge of the Harz Mountains and the Thuringian forests. Haunting the dark heights above the town, many believed, were witches and poltergeists. In the town churches, peasants and villagers took refuge against both threatening supernatural beings and natural hazards. The Luthers, among these other Saxons, needed such refuge. Tales of the Black Death, which had killed perhaps one-third of Europe's people, kept later generations aware of the precariousness of living and terrified when plaguelike diseases struck. Peasant existence and, for men like Hans, the mining business brought daily hazards. Thus, while a mine could yield copper and produce prosperity, it also might collapse on the miners or drag leaseholders like Hans into debt.

Pleading for all the help they could get, cowering believers prayed to saints. Miners invoked their popular protector St. Anne, known to them as the mother of the Virgin Mary. The pious, hoping such saints would shield them, feared a God who judged and punished them. To ward off the devil in such a setting, the Luther infant was brought just hours after his birth to Sts. Peter and Paul Church. There, after the saint of that day, they christened him Martin. The baptismal rite, though subdued, was momentous. The church taught that its waters cleansed the infant of sin as they drove out the devil and produced a new Christian.

Seven years after his baptism, his prudent parents sent Martin to Latin schools, first in his hometown of Mansfield, then in Magdeburg, and finally in Eisenach, for an experience that he later recounted as being in purgatory and hell. Those three schools were literally "trivial," which meant devoted to the trivium, because teachers drilled three subjects into the heads of urchins: Grammar served Luther well as he produced writings that now fill about one hundred mammoth volumes. Rhetoric, the second discipline, helped him become the influential writer and speaker whose words affronted and charmed multitudes for decades. The boy made much less of the third, logic, though it did help him survive philosophy courses later at the university.

In the Latin schools Martin also wrestled with Christian basics. If teachers taught also about the love of God, it was their warning that Jesus the Son of God would judge them after their death that fired their imaginations, especially Martin's. More alluring were Aesop's *Fables* and other stories that helped inform and prompt a mature Luther to salt his discourse with parables and narratives. In school Luther lived in terror of the "wolf," the classmate charged to tattle weekly on the children and finger them as candidates for physical punishment. But there were joys, as when young Martin savored the music that filled the chapel during Masses. Having learned to sing, the boys at Magdeburg and Eisenach performed during door-to-door rounds, welcoming "crumbs," or small gifts.

Influences that shaped the child remain obscure. He had several brothers and sisters and was close to one of them, Jacob, with whom he remembered playing. But he was very young when the burden of influence moved from home and family to school. The pious Brothers of the Common Life ran the school at Magdeburg and no doubt shared their love of the Scripture and the life of simple prayer with him. Some thought his known sightings of one begging Franciscan friar, formerly Prince Wilhelm of Anhalt, and his friendship with a learned priest at Eisenach inspired this alert adolescent when he later chose his vocation. Whatever young Luther might have been planning to study, father Hans insisted he take up law. Having a son who was an attorney or a judge would one day enhance the status and serve the practical needs of the aged Luthers.

He came to admire his teachers at Eisenach, so the Latin schools cannot have been such purgatories and hells as a scornful Luther later deemed them. So neither was his chosen university at Erfurt in Thuringia simply the whorehouse and beerhouse he would one day recall. In the summer of 1501, after taking his oath of loyalty to the dean, he launched a career that kept him in the university world all his life. Hans Luther's son was on track toward joining the Thuringian or Saxon elites through an academic career in a time when the fates of universities, the church, and civil governments were intertwined.

Luther used the university as his base as he developed his decisive role in the portentous intellectual, spiritual, and political dramas of his day. He remarked that the market town of Erfurt was a fortified city, so he felt protected there in many ways. Among the walled-in population of about twenty thousand lived almost a thousand priests, monks, and nuns. Faith was a public matter; the churchgoing citizens took Christian images from the sanctuaries to the streets, where townspeople enjoyed sacred processions, festivals, and displays of piety.

University authorities in Erfurt sternly regulated academic life. At four each morning the bell roused students for a day of rote learning and often wearying spiritual exercises. Starting low in class ranking, Luther studied hard and moved toward the top, usually enjoying his courses. He said he regarded the ceremonies that came with his master's degree—achieved in 1505—as incomparable among joys on earth, and he came to know enough joys to give weight to such a comparison.

While he followed his father's wishes and enrolled that year in legal studies, he almost instantly dropped out of them, explaining that in his mind law represented nothing but uncertainty. At Erfurt the edgy law professors liked to call theologians asses. Luther returned the compliment ever after by showing his disdain for lawyers. In the academy he now began to ask himself whether theology might offer him the certainty he was seeking in life, the assurance his soul and mind demanded, and a boon he could provide to others.

At Erfurt two living teachers and three dead philosophers especially caught his interest. Bartholomäus Arnoldi von Usingen and Jodocus Trutfetter were the professors who instructed Luther in the thought of the ancient thinker Aristotle and, from more recent centuries, William of Ockham and Gabriel Biel. Usingen and Trutfetter staged disputations, dead-serious debates, about their philosophies, ostensibly to seek truth. They taught students to be suspicious of even the greatest authors, men who might give the impression of being certain about assertions and claims when they were not or had no reason to be.

Luther determined along the way that when the philosophers considered human reason to be a credible agent for knowing and pleasing God they could offer none of the assurance of the love of God that he craved. As he studied philosophy he developed a lasting love-hate—from some angles even a hate-hate—relation to Aristotle. The Greek sage was a legitimate guide on practical earthly subjects, Luther affirmed, but he charged that Christian universities employed Aristotle's approach to reason as a deceptive and finally unsatisfying means for coming to know God.

Luther's professors, adapting what some called the modern way and others referred to as the nominalism of Ockham and Biel, stressed a commonsense counsel: Test theory by experience. For Luther, this meant questioning the writings of his teachers and then moving on to testing the absolute authority that the key institution, the church, claimed as the guardian of divine truth. Nominalists contended that only a particular, individual thing, not a general idea, was real. That meant humans could learn of a world beyond their everyday scene only through divine revelation, which is one reason why Scripture became so decisive for Luther and why he came to reject so much of the church's use of Aristotle's reason as a means of using ideas to find and please God.

Interrupting his academic course on a July day in 1505, the twenty-two-year-old graduate surprised friends and perhaps to some extent himself when he decided to trade academic garb for the cowl. He held a farewell supper for friends who then led him with tears, he said, to the door of the town's Black Cloister. With more than a tinge of melodrama he turned to pronounce, "This day you see me, and then, not ever again." Friends had to ask why he made this sudden decision. One acquaintance blamed Luther's apparently abrupt move on the melancholy he displayed after the death of two friends. Another faulted the supernatural, musing that an apparition must have visited him. His father, who thought Martin was now going to waste his education, his life, and the prospects of his parents, was predictably furious.

Luther later admitted that fear turned him to his new course. On the way back to the university after a journey home on July 2, as he neared the village of Stotternheim, he was jolted by a thunderbolt and lightning. "Help me, St. Anne," he prayed, and then vowed, "I will become a monk." He busied himself with interpreting this event all his life.

Sixteen years later he wrote to his father that he had that summer day been called by terrors from heaven. Specifically, cowering in the agony of prospective sudden death and the dread of divine judgment, he made the monastic vow he thought he could never break. Soon he was called to prostrate himself before an altar at Erfurt, over the brass plate that covered a tomb. Buried there was an Augustinian leader who in 1415 at a church council in Constance had helped condemn to death the prophetic Bohemian preacher Jan Hus. Ironically, Luther and others came later to honor not the buried Augustinian but his victim Hus as a precedent for their own ventures, a martyr to true faith and a man who defied those spiritual rulers who turned him over to secular authorities for execution.

The custodians of the cloister doors that closed behind Luther on July 17 belonged to the very strict Order of Augustinian Hermits. Luther selected his order well, since Augustinians prized scholarship, as did he. They honored and studied the fifth-century scholar and bishop St. Augustine, as would he. He was ready for self-punishing treatment, and they offered it. Monastery rules demanded that the novice master, the prior, and other chapter leaders must regiment the lives of monks. Luther dutifully obeyed, but though he had sought rigor, he came to chafe under the weight of the monotonous routines. Years later he disparaged the monastic disciplines as distractions from what he determined the fear-stricken and spiritually hungry people of God deserved.

Beyond the walls of the university, the fortifications of Erfurt, and then the protective confines of the cloister, the world around Luther was in turmoil, and he was soon to find himself unexpectedly central to much of its drama. We know almost nothing about what he knew or thought about the political and religious conflict of the moment, but one of its features had to stand out: His was an entirely Catholic world. After Spain had defeated the Muslims and purged the Jews in 1492, Europe became almost solely Christian, and Christianity was the only faith recognized and supported by the governments. Christians did not live near the people they called the Turk, Muslims with whom they were in imperial conflict. Small Jewish communities mainly under force and sometimes partly by choice still huddled in Italian ghettos or clustered around synagogues in numerous towns of northern Europe. Mountain valleys hid a few dissenting Christian sectarians. While folk beliefs that the theologians of the day called pagan were very widespread, a Christian could roam through Europe and find familiar the main beliefs of almost anyone he met. By the time Luther died, however, even the surface unity of Western Christendom would be shattered. What he learned in the university and how he used that learning contributed decisively to the shattering.

To help make sense of Luther's inner world, his thought, and the emphases in his subsequent career therefore requires some acts of imagination. I like to picture someone from any remote culture where people did not worship God stumbling onto the monastic scene and being utterly bewildered. Such a person from beyond Christendom in those years might well have comprehended the new sciences then developing in Europe, but the form that the search for meaning took and the theology used to interpret it would have been alien and forbidding. Luther, like the poets Chaucer and Dante before him and like the scholars Desiderius Erasmus and Thomas More in his own time, inhabited a spiritual world in which people struggled in inventive ways with God and Satan, going on pilgrimages and fearing purgatories. Their religious ventures taught them to be consumed by the threat of damnation and the hope of being saved for eternity with God.

Luther boasted that if ever a pious monk could have gotten to heaven through his monkery, it would have been he. He said he prayed, fasted, kept vigils, and almost froze to death in the unheated chambers. Though his colleagues evidently considered him a good friar, he confessed that he faced persistent temptations. These were not beguilingly sexual, and little in his record would attract those with prurient tastes. As he wrestled against the lures of the devil, he instead became increasingly convinced that no one could ever do what he fervently aspired to do, that is, please God through monastic efforts. Their hours spent in solitude gave Augustinians ample time to explore the inner life. Luther testified that from the first he struggled with himself and his God. The proper dealing with a God of wrath and love and the search for certitude in God's relation to humans became the grand themes of his life. Explain his life story as one will, it makes sense chiefly as one rooted in and focused by what has to be called an obsession with God: God present and God absent, God too near and God too far, the God of wrath and the God of love, God weak and God almighty, God real and God as illusion, God hidden and God revealed.

On April 4, 1507, a bishop ordained Martin a priest. Then on May 2 twenty horses and twenty horsemen made up the guest party of father Hans Luther, who arrived at Erfurt carrying twenty gulden to donate on the day of Martin's first Mass. The cloister enclosure, the miles between old home and new monastery, and enduring bitter feelings had kept father and son apart. Now for Martin this day was to be the most portentous since his baptism. Since the presence of Hans threatened to turn celebration into trauma, it is natural to ask why the father appeared at all. Guilt and fear after the death of two friends in the plague prompted him, thought some. Maybe he held himself responsible for their deaths because he had long spurned his son's God-pleasing vocation. Or, moved by a puzzling if prudent change of mind, he could have come to show newly found pride in his priestly son. Then again, he could have been merely keeping a parental obligation. Perhaps he hoped against hope that the two would be reconciled. Whatever the reason, the father was ostentatiously present.

When newly ordained priests celebrated Mass for the first time, they were made aware of the privilege they gained therewith to offer God the sacrificial gifts of bread and wine. Those who partook of the prescribed meal at the altar believed that they ingested not bread and wine but the body and blood of Jesus Christ. Such a ritual naturally inspired awe. Luther rehearsed the precise and complex motions of the rite as he learned them from a textbook. Still, mixed feelings about his unworthiness to hold Christ's body and to pour his blood came to overwhelm him. How dared he, sinful monk Martin, presume to talk directly to God, to represent the people, and to create the impression that he was worthy to participate in the change of bread to flesh, wine to blood?

Though filled with dread, he survived the ordeal. At a celebration after Mass Hans Luther chose the moment to interrogate his cornered son: What if that thunderstorm at Stotternheim and your call to the monastery came from the devil? Hans then turned catechist and asked his son standard questions about the Fourth Commandment: Have you not heard that you are to honor father and mother? Had this son not disobeyed God when he dishonored his own parents by his choice to go against their strong wishes and enter the monastery? It is not known if Luther responded, though on occasion he later referred to the questions that had to sear his soul.

Luther showed a need for a new figure to act as father, since his dealing with his own parent was strained and his life behind cloister walls kept the two remote from each other. He found one in his Augustinian superior, the blue-blooded Vicar General Johannes von Staupitz. Well positioned, Staupitz had significant influence on his longtime friend Frederick the Wise of Saxony. Frederick was titled Elector because he was one of seven secular and ecclesiastical princes who elected the Holy Roman Emperor.

Staupitz showed himself to be an astute talent scout when in 1508 he sent young scholar Luther to be substitute professor of moral philosophy in the backwater Saxon burg of Wittenberg. While the local bishop was opposed to the idea and the church did not charter it, Frederick in 1502 had started a university there, a place that Luther described as existing at the edge of barbarism. The school originally had to settle for second-rate talent, so the elector and Staupitz wanted to upgrade it.

Staupitz early recognized Luther's abilities. For example, he assigned the monk the task of helping reconcile two quarreling Augustinian factions. That duty meant a trek to headquarters in Rome. When in November of 1510 or 1511, after having crossed the Alps on foot, the impressionable young monk first saw the holy city, he gasped in awe but, curiously, thereafter recorded few observations about the grand sights. Unmoved when he glimpsed the ancient Pantheon, by then converted to a church, he commented not on classic examples of architecture but on the evils of paganism.

After his four business-filled weeks in Rome, he even

withheld comment on the splendor of the city's seven great churches. A crawl through the catacombs, described to him as burial places for thousands of early Christian martyrs, did lead him to be stirred. Like many other northern European visitors, he expressed shock at the chaos, the filth, and the practices of locals who urinated in public and openly patronized prostitutes. Priests appeared to him to be ignorant and corrupt functionaries who scorned the pious, profanely raced through their obligatory Masses, and blasphemously hurried Luther through those he celebrated.

He dared not let the Roman days pass, however, without seeking to satisfy his spiritual thirst. He heard that the merits he would accrue by venerating saintly relics or by saying Masses would shorten the number of years his own parents would have to spend suffering in purgatory. He later revealed that he had wished they were already dead, so their future sins would not nullify his efforts at getting all their transgressions purged. Climactically, on his knees at the Lateran Palace he climbed the Santa Scala, then believed to be the very stairs brought to Rome from Jerusalem, steps that Jesus had himself climbed in the court of Pontius Pilate fifteen centuries earlier. On each step Luther said a stipulated prayer. When he had finally made his way to the top, a question nagged at him: "Who knows whether this is really true?" This is the moment in Rome that he would speak and write about in a sermon more than thirty years later.

Luther and a companion who made the round-trip by foot over the Alps in winter returned to Wittenberg to report on a failed mission, but his superiors did not lose confidence in him. In October of 1512 under a pear tree in the cloister garden, Staupitz astonished the still uncertain monk by ordering him to receive the doctorate and thence to serve the Augustinian congregation of monks in Wittenberg as a teacher of theology and by preaching. No, the twenty-six-year-old Luther at first protested, he had already spent so many energies that he did not expect to live long. Further, only those more gifted and older than he should preach and be doctoral teachers. One lure about the offer, however, did attract him. He would be teaching Scripture and would no longer have to take on the dreaded task of expounding Aristotle's *Nicomachean Ethics*. He obeyed orders, overcame his doubts about the assignment, and proudly accepted the doctorate on October 19 that year. He often said that he would not exchange his doctorate for all the world's gold, since he saw it as a call and commission to his work and because it gave him courage. Since some jealous colleagues at his alma mater in Erfurt, where he had taught briefly, sneered that his rapid rise in the academy resulted from favoritism, he was happy not to make Erfurt his permanent home. He found good reason to respond positively when Staupitz assigned him again to Wittenberg, where the vicar general cajoled Elector Frederick into underwriting his protégé's stipend.

The young monk and Staupitz, who became his confessor, inhabited a universe in which they thought a threatening God kept a suspicious eye on every human act. While the confessor appeared to Luther to have figured out a way to live under this weight, uncertainty about God's will for him terrified Luther. He quickly became a virtuoso self-examiner, boring his mentor during six-hour confession sessions. A genius at probing reasons for his own hidden resistance to God, he grew dependent and later said that without the help of Staupitz, his venerable father in Christ, he would have remained a papal ass, doomed to be swallowed up in hell.

His weary mentor berated Luther for making do at confession with what he called flummery and pseudo faults, as if calling every fart a sin. Luther in turn averred that he was confessing not the usual monkish transgressions about sexual temptations, but what he called knots, spiritually serious problems. Staupitz often was of help as his protégé wrestled with these knotty phobias and specters. He discerned that the dread of death or hell, the apparent ultimate challenges, indicated in Luther a still deeper torment, a fear of God, a failure to know the love of God in Luther's inmost heart, and an inability to be certain about the promises of God.

Explicit rules for the rite of confession began with the demand that the sinner be contrite. That sounded like a simple idea—to be contrite meant to be sorry for sins, as Luther was—but he rendered it complex. Since the monk wanted a pure relation with God, it struck him that even being sorry could mean being self-centered. Through contrition a person could seek advantage by proving to God that he could cooperate in the steps he climbed to please God. Luther instead began a lifelong search for ways in which humans could experience the love of God without using God, without turning God into a convenience. Felicitously he borrowed from Augustine an image that helped him describe the central problem about humans. Even while being contrite, he noticed, they would be "curved in" upon themselves, cramped, protective, in no way open for God to break into their souls. Curved in upon himself, he lived with the terrors that marked his moves within the dreary cloister walls. Of his experience there he later said that he feared hell somewhat; death, more; failure to please God the judge who made drastic demands, most: "I trembled."

Somehow he came to conceive that repenting, turning from sin, should begin with a focus on the love of God and not of the self. He next had to reject what his teachers in the modern way had taught him in their precise formula: "To those who do what lies within them, God does not deny grace." He faced a nagging issue: How could he be certain that he was doing his best and that his best was good enough to appease God? Luther called this question a figurative thunderbolt from heaven which matched the real bolt that had knocked him down and directed him to the monastery. Stunned to realize that an angry God was demanding what no human, however saintly, could accomplish, he raged before Staupitz. His superior and confessor in turn chided him, observing that, no, God was not angry with Luther; the monk was angry with God.

In his next dread-filled step toward the release for which he strove, Luther pondered a Creator who obviously chose to show favor only to some creatures, displaying a divine generosity that reached no one but the elect of God. The logic was compelling: The God who chose some had to be the one who rejected the rest. How could a person square this action with the claim that God was a God of love?

Staupitz evidently seemed at ease, doubtless regarding himself among the chosen. Such self-confidence was beyond Luther. Staupitz reached into the depths of Catholic understanding when he told Luther not to concentrate on the terrible judgments of an inscrutable God. No, what mattered at this stage of his striving was what the sinner could always easily count on, the wounds of Christ and thus the love of God. "Wounds" referred to Jesus' death for others on the cross, which in the New Testament stories was the scene of divine rescue.

So much then for release from being curved in upon himself. Luther's search for certainty, however, led him to ask a second question: On whose authority does one know that all this is true for him? His confessor appealed to the authority of the church, but Luther was growing discontented with its answers. Another authority instead increasingly appealed to him: the Scripture, which he found to be a more sure provider of answers. Commissioned to teach the Bible as the revelation of God, he now scoured the book for assurance that the church's teachings on reconciliation with God were true. As he came to see that he did not have to be only curved in upon himself but could also be free from the arbitrary authority of the church, he was still uncertain about how the scriptural word applied to him personally.

His way of dealing with his personal questions intersected with political upheavals that at first seemed remote but that enabled him eventually to make an impact on the world from his provincial base in and near Saxony and Thuringia, and especially in the forlorn little town of Wittenberg that now demands our attention. Luther's earliest and most vicious biographer, Johannes Cochlaeus, described the town as it appeared in 1524, twelve years after Luther settled there, as small, poor, ugly, stinking, hideous, wretched, unhealthy, smoky, full of slop, populated by barbarians and sellers of beer and not by real citizens. He went on to take note of the unfinished fledgling university, the castle, and an Augustinian chapter house. Apart from these, the jaundiced author noted nothing except homes of Luther devotees, which to him meant filthy houses on filthy streets.

A year after Luther arrived, the town housed perhaps 2,100 people. In 172 of about 400 houses and huts, residents owned licenses to brew beer, but beyond that they produced little and marketed less. Fortunately for the spread of work by Luther and his colleagues, the town boasted a new printing press, a recent invention that helped disseminate literary products from the university, which placed Wittenberg on the mind of Rome and the map of Europe.

Some in the church saw that there was money to be made even though the populace was not wealthy. Notably, Elector Frederick the Wise stocked the Castle Church and the church of the All Saints Foundation with moneymaking attractions in the form of relics said to be objects surviving from biblical times. His inventory in 1518 catalogued 17,443 items, including the thumb of St. Anne, a twig of the burning bush that Moses had witnessed, some thorns from Jesus' crown, hay stalks from Christ's manger, some milk of the

Virgin Mary, and a whole corpse of one child plus a couple of hundred body parts of other innocent infant victims massacred by King Herod's soldiers after the birth of Jesus. Residents and visitors who paid money to venerate these relics believed their devotion resulted in a contract assuring that God would deduct centuries from the time they would have had to suffer in the flames of purgatory after death. One devout and expensive visit to these relics in 1520 could help a sinner escape from such suffering for precisely 1,902,202 years and 270 days. Luther was among those taught to gain assurance from venerating relics, the yield from which meant profit for Frederick.

After the Wittenberg faculty admitted Luther in October 1512, he set to work probing the text of older commentaries on Genesis and then studied the Psalms, already familiar because he had memorized them in monastic disciplines and worship. He also kept drawing on the learning of humanists, whom he had read with care, but now he also turned to a second group of writers. These were mystics, among them the Dominican monk Johannes Tauler (d. 1361), along with the anonymous author of *A German Theology*. Such benign spiritual aspirants strove to forge a union of the human soul with God. While the promise of such union was alluring, Luther thought that in the mystics it relied too much on human striving, since to be effective it depended on a divine spark in the soul. If such a spark existed, he thought it could never lead to an achievement that would reassure mortals who wanted to be free from bondage to sin and the fear of death. A holy God, he thought, could never tolerate intimacy with humans who, despite their sincere ambitions, inevitably remained unholy.

Not all his reading of the mystics was a loss. From them he learned to be ready for storms along the spiritual journey, clouds that in his writing on Romans he called dark shadows. He especially plundered the insights of those mystics who viewed God not only as an aloof power but also as someone who, though still hidden, was close to humans in their suffering. From these spiritual ancestors he further learned the virtue of passivity, which meant turning over decisive matters of the soul to the God who was, he thought, at the same time both absent and revealed. Taken together, however, these mystical teachings were not yet satisfying.

In simplest terms, Luther found the mystics trying to pursue their union with God at God's level, which he considered by definition to be beyond human reach. Confessor Staupitz instead was leading the young searcher to enjoy union with an approachable God who condescended to the human level, while an unknown divine Being high in majesty was inaccessible. In Luther's reasoning, mortals would have to discern and experience God in the known, especially in those wounds of a loving Christ. He avidly read Paul the apostle, who pointed to Jesus on the cross, preaching that God's activity in that instance was designed to reach and rescue him from uncertain existence and terror of punishment.

The glosses that Luther scribbled on the margins of his Scripture and gleanings from student notations taken in class at six in the morning reveal stages along his path of development. Teacher Luther showed that from the first he was not a dispassionate commentator but instead someone who engaged in high-stakes contests with the God of the Bible. On one level, true, he was a scholar within an academic discipline. Thanks to the achievements of contemporary humanists who were revisiting ancient languages and editing texts, he joined the company of those who were rescuing the Bible from the relative neglect it had long suffered. With their aid he mastered Hebrew and Greek as he turned to what they and he called the grammatical or literal approach to the biblical text. Long-favored allegorical methods had given interpreters too much leeway into fantasy. The no-nonsense approach instead made the stark meanings and brunt of the texts inescapable.

Since Scripture was now clear, reading it made him shudder, because he could not personally dodge the demands of the God that he found in it. So he plundered the letters of the apostle Paul, the oldest surviving documents of Christian faith. In 1515 and 1516, as he studied and taught Paul's letters to the Romans and Galatians, praying and wrestling with God, he concluded that the Bible often reinforced the pictures in his mind of a holy, zealous, wrathful, and punishing God whose scrutinizing eye was always on all mortals, including Doctor Luther.

The church helped him make efforts to please God, but his efforts all left him drastically short of his reach. God the enemy could annihilate him or any other selfish soul still curved in upon itself even while in the act of seeking God. Luther therefore emerged from his study as both a scholar and a sufferer. He complained of insomnia and constipation, bad enough external symptoms, but the turbulence in his soul was unbearable. He was wrestling with God, but his use of reason and the piling up of human merits were, in his eye, futile and even destructive.

So engrossing, to some tortuous, was Luther's spiritual pilgrimage that it is tempting to see him as a solitary genius or uniquely troubled soul. Anything but that. Had he been an isolated searcher his effort would not have been alluring to so many others, and word of his teaching would not have attracted such a large following within less than a decade. In his time, while many records reveal spiritual sluggishness among the masses, multitudes of other earnest monks and scholars, priests and pious Christian folk were also strenuously seeking the favor of God. In their private struggles, however, none of them influenced both the personal existence and the public life of others as Luther did.

His psyche, a rich lode for students who mine the deeps of conflicted human experience, exposes a fundamental and in many ways very curious feature in his testimony: The experience of God for him was uncommonly vivid, but the God revealed was at the same time hidden. God was not clearly accessible through philosophy, the study of nature, the efforts of good works, or the union offered in mysticism. Luther eventually came to experience this God as one who came not in power but in weakness, shrouded in the form of the helpless infant Jesus or the dying figure of Christ as a criminal on the cross.

The interplay between these two apprehensions of God

was unremitting. The hidden God had to be unappealing to anyone who struggled for certainty. Yet this was the same God declared to be surely accessible in scriptural stories and preaching, in sacramental bread and wine and water, in the community called the church, as the compassionate one who kept at heart the best interests of humans.

With every discovery Luther found a new complication, including the most troubling of all. This God hidden and revealed, according to clear biblical texts, condemned many but saved few. Therefore, thought Luther, this must be a cruel God who made arbitrary choices among creatures. Yet people who in faith and trust enjoyed the sacraments and heard the Word were told that they received the love of God in their inmost hearts. How could this be? He would eventually resolve some of these apparent contradictions in talking about God, but at this point the God who stunned Luther the frightened traveler on the road in a thunderstorm or in the monastery silence was a threat to his very being.

When the two aspects of God came to conflict in Luther's soul, he used a word that does not translate well, *Anfechtungen*, the spiritual assaults that he said kept people from finding certainty in a loving God. He was sure that the nagging, even horrifying *Anfechtungen* that assaulted him as a young professor and then lifelong were a plague to everyone, and that he must help rescue others. *Anfechtungen* attacked with a voice that came during what he called the night battles in the dark chambers of the cloister and of his soul. This inner voice echoed the one that haunted him on the sacred steps back in Rome: "Who knows whether this is really true?" No

longer did being true refer to some statements about the au-
thenticity of relics or issues of historical verification but instead, much more seriously, to the existence or reality of
God. Each person who wanted and needed to find and be
found right with a gracious God must struggle. It had become clear that Luther did not hunger merely for the experience of grace but, still and always, behind and beyond it,
for assurance and certainty.

Since *Anfechtungen* were rooted in profound doubt, Luther
thought that the alluring world and the devil had to be the
immediate agents of the taunting. But—and this was much
more disturbing—since God was the final determiner of everything, God must either be the stage manager for the drama
of doubt or the main actor in causing it. Whenever he reflected on this, Luther said he was left without hope in an
abyss of despair. Curiously, he also came later to say that
even when he despaired he was concurrently given grace to
probe ever more deeply and, in each encounter, to find a way
to discern a profound divine purpose. He wrote that he
found that God provoked *Anfechtungen* as if in an embrace
and called *Anfechtungen* "delicious despair." Such despair offered sinners opportunities to grow in faith. The assaults
robbed them of all certainty, until they found no place to go
except to the God of mercy and grace.

Had Luther not eventually come to display and preach
confidence in the promises of God, not many of the thousands who shared his pilgrimage of faith or who were
cheered and guided by his message and program would have
followed. He would have been lost to history, one more for-

gotten, distraught soul. Yet he did find fresh ways to speak of this double experience of doubt and victory. The best example out of hundreds appeared in his comments on the biblical patriarch Jacob. These were remarks he made in classes and lectures late in life, preserved in not fully reliable notes by students and then published as commentaries on Genesis. In many ways these frame his spiritual autobiography, especially concerning his *Anfechtungen.*

I am going to linger over these comments and quote Luther liberally here, because they provide so much perspective. He would talk about Jacob but in many ways he was also *being* Jacob, who in the biblical story wrestled through the night at a ford in the brook Jabbok. Toward morning, as neither struggler could prevail, after the foe struck Jacob in the thigh, dislocating his hip, he asked to be let go. Jacob would not release this other figure unless he got a blessing, which he did finally receive—along with the new name Israel.

Jabbok was remote in time and place from Wittenberg, so the Jacob that Luther observed wrestling at the brook correlates to the monk struggling in the monastery. Anxiety, terror, weakness, solitude, and temptation, he wrote, come most fiercely at night. God, he went on, "at times is accustomed to play with his saints" in "quite childish ways." The fight of Jacob, Luther wrote, was "not against flesh, blood, the devil, and a good angel but against God appearing in hostile form."

Here Luther made a leap from the Genesis story in the Hebrew Scripture, the Old Testament, to the Christian story in the New Testament. He characteristically fused the plots of both testaments. So it could be that *ish*, the Hebrew word for man, the wrestling foe, was for him at the same time also "our Lord Jesus Christ, eternal God and future Man." To him, the Jacob who would not let go was insisting, "I have the promise of God." For Luther this was the equivalent of the Christian realization "I am baptized."

The faith of Jacob through the night, like that of Luther through the years, paradoxically was very weak and likewise very strong, he noted. Luther advised believers: "So you should reflect: 'I am not alone in being tempted concerning the wrath of God, predestination, and unbelief.'" All the saints experienced the same. Now in the Jacob story he stressed one special line: *"In this passage it is expressly stated: 'You have prevailed with God,' not only 'you have striven with God' but 'you have also conquered.'"*

Fortunately for assessors of Luther's orthodoxy and appraisers of his sanity, he at once acknowledged that "it seems absurd that we are called lords and conquerors of God. And this is certainly true if we judge according to philosophy. But in the Spirit and in theology it is right and godly to say that God is conquered by us." So Luther proudly coined a proverb about the wrestling hold: "When you think that our Lord God has rejected a person, you should think that our Lord God has him in His arms and is pressing him to His heart." Here was a conquered but still wrestling God with "his omnipotence concealed. God conquered has surrendered and is bound to and by the divine promise." Luther was not trying to be heretical when he dealt with divine power. God, he added, "is not conquered in such a way that He is subjected to us, but His judgment, or His wrath and fury and whatever opposes us, is conquered by us by praying, seeking, and knocking, so that from an angry judge, as He seemed to be previously, He becomes a most loving Father."

Everything in the wrestling match depended on faith, Luther added, "for this is the highest sacrifice, not to cease praying and seeking until we conquer [God]. He has already surrendered Himself to us that we may be certain of victory, for He has bound Himself to His promises and pledges his faithfulness with an oath." Monk Martin was later to advise many on the basis of this personal experience: "I have often seen excellent men horribly vexed by terrors, afflictions, and the severest persecutions, so much so that they nearly experienced despair of heart. But these things must be learned so that we may be able to comfort such men and interpret the temptations as the special manner by which God is accustomed to wrestle with us in the form of a destroyer and that we may exhort them firmly to retain the promise, or lamp and spark, of the Word in the hope that the rescue will certainly follow."

While his thoughts on wrestling and conquering God and on the experience of divine grace were still developing—we have his word for it—Luther began to go public with that experience and with his study as these related to the culture of church and empire. What followed was a clash between those on the one hand who believed that they could be right with God through chiefly external means such as pilgrimages, rituals, visiting relics, and paying for Masses, and those on the other who hungered for internal means which would produce truly changed hearts and help them realize inwardly the experience of God. The hierarchy, from the pope down to the local priest, controlled the first of these. They could excommunicate anyone and deny the Mass and thus heaven to those who disobeyed them.

It happened that all these met challenge from a significant number of territorial and national rulers who chafed under such threats and who were seeking secular power. Spain, France, and England, beginning to cohere as nations, became powerful enough to challenge the Papal States and the allies of the pope, who also had grand ambition and a lust for temporal power. These rulers were not spiritually free from the papal domain, but through a shifting pattern of alliances they were weakening the pope's temporal reign, reducing him to something like monarchical status and forcing him to make many compromises. It was on this scene that, when Luther was to make his challenge to Rome, the pope would not know how to counter him or, if he made moves to do so, would not be free for reasons of political alliance easily to close in and exterminate him.

The common people and not a few of their magistrates and princes had begun to focus on the inner needs and resources of people. In much of Europe there was evidence that crowds were asking for a personal relation to a loving Christ. To that end they attended to devotions, prayed, joined movements to stimulate spirituality, and tried to find means to ward off death and the devil in a time of great hazards from plague, economic change, and the like. Many of them reacted to priestly scandal and corrupt politics by becoming openly anticlerical. Sculptures of the pope being thrown into hell could be found in churches. Many people disrespected priests, monks, and nuns and were ready to turn from them. Their hungers matched that of Luther, even if they were less gifted than he at speaking up. Attacking the priestly and sacramental system was Luther's first move; assaulting the official church and questioning its divine authority came next.

In 1517, everything that Luther was beginning to discover about righteousness and faith collided with the Roman church's system as it found most blatant expression in his Saxon neighborhood through the activities of one Johannes Tetzel. That Dominican had no difficulty filling the role of the heavy in all stories of young Luther. A gifted preacher and a superior salesperson, he used his moonlighting role as an inquisitor to intimidate opponents even as he peddled instruments that he claimed offered sinners spiritual release. Proceeds from his sales went to Pope Leo X in Rome, Arch bishop Albrecht in Mainz, and Tetzel himself.

Albrecht, already archbishop of Magdeburg, in 1514 additionally purchased the archbishop title in Mainz. He thereby went into deep debt to the Fugger banking family of Augsburg in order to pay Rome, which charged money for such benefices. Naturally, he and the Fuggers backed Tetzel's enterprise. The pope did not dare send the most aggressive marketers of holy goods into rival Spain, France, or England, so he was reduced to working with Albrecht. That archbishop welcomed the income even as he risked reaction of the sort Luther was soon to provide and which many in the general public supported.

Licensed and unfettered, Tetzel could raise significant funds while deluding the spiritually hungry with scams, building resentment against a money-grubbing church. He sold certificates called indulgences, leniencies, or generosities. Sinners who paid money received a writ saying that they did not have to make satisfaction for their sins or suffer in purgatory. Western Christians had long been subject to a system of penance in which contrite and forgiven sinners had to make satisfaction for the harm done by their sins. The penance system especially fit the ethos of northern Europeans, who had made much of the notion of restitution. They were told that to be purged of the enduring effects of sin they had to make up for past offenses in this world or, in much greater pain, after death in flaming purgatory. God, however, would grant special favors to those who were ready to pay.

Church leaders advertised indulgences by propagating the idea that Jesus gave to Peter and hence his papal successors the power either to loose or to bind sinners. Loosing them left them right with God, ready for heaven. Binding them kept them long in purgatory. Jesus and the saints, however, had so pleased God that they piled up extra merits in a sort of treasury. The pope could authorize dipping into that treasury and applying bonus amounts to the accounts of the penitent sinners on earth or of those already suffering in purgatory. For a price, the owners of indulgences could see their time in purgatory shortened. Critics asked why, if the pope had the power to shorten purgatorial suffering, he did not do it free of charge. The pope did not have to answer such impertinent questions.

Because anguished sinners made pilgrimages to revere the holy relics in his giant collection, a practice for which they made gifts or paid money, Elector Frederick the Wise regarded the indulgences authorized by Albrecht and sold by Tetzel to be costly competitors. Since Frederick banned indulgence sellers from his territory, Tetzel had to market beyond the borders. Wittenbergers, for example, had to travel eighteen miles to make purchases from him. Luther the Saxon naively assumed that the pope, distant in Rome and probably not aware of the scene near Wittenberg, would applaud his efforts to correct the abuses which climaxed in the indulgence system. He thought that informed and shocked church authorities would come to regard Tetzel's beguiling preaching as blasphemy. The Dominican's approach, Luther reasoned, could cause torture in the minds of the poor or the pinched. They had to ask themselves how they would dare to subject their parents and others to sufferings in purgatory if they could have chosen to pay Tetzel for indulgences to shorten their time there.

In the autumn of 1517, still thinking he could work within the official church system, Luther somewhat ingenuously appealed to his own bishop and to Archbishop Albrecht to take their responsibilities seriously. The scandalous indulgence system, he charged, was dangerous to the exploited Saxon people. He stated the case starkly in a treatise, claiming that these practices took away from men the fear of God and handed them over to the wrath of God. He worried that those who purchased letters of indulgence would become complacent about their situation before God. They would feel that they could sin and not fear purgatorial punishment.

Since bishops like Albrecht and the pope authorized indulgences, Luther posed what he had determined because of his own agonies vis-à-vis the good offices of the bishops: "No man can be assured of his salvation by any episcopal function." The apostle Paul had ordered believers to work out their own salvation "constantly 'in fear and trembling.'" Who would tremble with a letter of indulgence in his pocket? Luther hoped that an aware young Albrecht would execute what he called the first and only duty of the bishops, which was to see that people learn the gospel and the love of Christ.

To advance his claims, the young professor sent a letter to Albrecht and enclosed some theses to begin to make this central case. Luther denigrated himself as a humble feces of a human being, while he exalted his superior. As if to mark a turn in his vocation, he signed his letter no longer Martinus Ludher or Luder but Luther, just as sometimes in writing to colleagues he now dipped into Latin for a pun, calling himself Eleutherius. Like Jacob who received the new name Israel, Luther with such usage gave himself a name that meant "the free one."

The document that went along with the letter to Albrecht became the 95 Theses, which Luther either nailed to the door at the Castle Church in Wittenberg or sent to Mainz, or both. As theses of this sort were unfinished products, designed to provoke debate, Luther asked for and scheduled an academic disputation. Not a single person showed up for it. The theses stood a good chance of being forgotten as most other such propositions for debate have been. It may be that the junior faculty at Wittenberg had already grown used to such debates, were perhaps a bit bored by the subject, or were ready to take such revolutionary theses for granted. The common people, illiterate in Latin, would not yet have been reached and stirred.

Tetzel, however, reacted in fury. He inflamed the Dominicans to pursue this noxious irritant through disputation and by tattling to Rome. Prince-Archbishop Albrecht was also nettled by the man he disdained as the impudent monk at Wittenberg. He had other distractions on his mind, though, and wanted to avoid stirring disputes among Dominicans and Augustinians. He dared not use this affront to antagonize his despised rival Frederick the Wise, who, he knew, would protect Luther.

As Rome received more and more notices of the monkish squabbles, officials for a time vastly underestimated the appeal of Luther and the power of a growing number of his colleagues. As for the three main church figures by then involved, Tetzel the inquisitor had the power to complicate Luther's life, Albrecht possessed authority to have someone who challenged the church reprimanded, and Pope Leo X could have Luther condemned on the basis of new declarations of authority.

Near the end of the Fifth Lateran Council in 1516, Pope Leo X in a formal papal document called a bull asserted that the pope had the power and right and full authority to call, adjourn, and dissolve the councils of bishops. He contended: "It is necessary for the salvation of all souls that all Christian believers be subject to the pope at Rome." This, Leo added, was done "for the benefit of the unity and power of the church which has been entrusted to him." This declaration was perfectly timed to deal with Luther's challenge to that unity and his power.

Only a few students could hear Luther teach and only a few hundred townspeople in Wittenberg or at stops along his way could hear him preach. Thousands across Europe, however, now read him and gathered their own impressions. With or without permission, printers greedily snapped up and published the young monk's pronouncements. Luther was adept, even brilliant, at exploiting the new medium that was developing rapidly after Johannes Gutenberg of Nuremberg invented movable metal type for printing presses. Admitting or joking that he delivered as soon as he conceived, Luther found his words transcribed and distributed, and never received a penny of the yield. He did well in the bargain, since the publications attracted ever more support to his developing cause.

Europeans thus generally had to make up their minds about Luther as writer, not as preacher. While most people of the time were still illiterate, city dwellers of influence who could and did read him helped articulate his message beyond their company of readers. For various reasons, no one immediately exercised effective authority against him. Luther took advantage of the moment, as did the printers who got their hands on the theses which Luther had sent in longhand to Albrecht. As they published the documents, people rallied against the practice of transporting money to Rome and the system of penance. Luther was not happy at first to learn that copies of his theses were being widely published and sold. Though he had sounded cocksure, he was also a virtuoso questioner who confessed to having had certain doubts about some of the 95. Had he foreseen the sensational follow-up, he explained, he would have been more careful in some statements.

Tetzel, playing copycat, came up with 106 forgettable theses defending the papacy and casting Luther as someone dangerous to the official church, which by now he was. More important, the skilled debater Johannes Eck of Ingolstadt, who had access to power on the highest levels, now began to counter the Wittenberger. For the next four years Luther defined and defended himself in this tense atmosphere. He could not turn back. Almost from the beginning commentators agreed that his theses and other teachings had the potential to shake the church and thus significantly alter the Western Christian world. Luther later described his action as an assault on the heavens and a setting of the world afire, and in the context of Europe in that day he was not far off the mark.

In neither the covering letter nor the theses did Eleutherius free himself of all old assumptions or leave behind loyalties to the church, the pope, or the clergy. He did argue, however, that popes and priests did not hold the keys to open and close the door of purgatory or the power to shorten one's time there. Since no official dogma defined indulgences, Luther was still within the bounds of orthodoxy as he criticized the exploiters who sold them. He sounded almost exuberant in his 62nd Thesis, which suggested: "The true treasure of the church is the most holy gospel of the glory and grace of God."

Theses at the beginning and the end of the document were aimed to rouse his enemies to action and lead many others in Europe to begin to look with hope for freedom from the system. Penance was a churchly invention. God wanted something else, as Thesis 1 asserted: "When our Lord and Master Jesus Christ said, 'Repent' [Matt. 4:17], he willed the entire life of believers to be one of repentance." That biblical word could never refer to penance as administered by the clergy. Repentance—turning, being turned by God—had to be first inner and then outward. It must produce effects that would lead a person to make humble confession and be ready for both a change in a way of life and receipt of the gift of the glory and grace of God.

Here was not professor or doctor but pastor Luther caring for souls, including his own. Though death and hell still threatened, Luther wrote in climactic theses: "Christians should be exhorted to be diligent in following Christ, their head, through penalties, death, and hell" so that they might finally "thus be confident of entering into heaven through many tribulations rather than through the false security of penance [Acts 14:22]."

Something was still missing in Luther's wrestling with the issues of repentance and grace. He remained uncertain as to whether the benign face of God ever beamed into *his* hungry soul. He remained certain that an angry God still confronted him and left him without true assurance. In a few pages of autobiography that he penned in his last year, Luther revisited the story of the basic turn that he took when he was young. Not always consistent or accurate about chronological details in his several reminiscences, he wrote in this memoir that his discovery had occurred in 1519. More likely it was late in 1517 or early in 1518. Whenever it occurred, it is clear that he had anticipated it over a period of several years. Since it is difficult enough for moderns to gain access to a worldview that led to a spiritual revolution over two words, *righteousness* and *faith*, it is helpful to pay attention to his autobiographical accounting.

He remembered that he was jolted into his new understanding while in the heated little Black Cloister tower-study that was a perquisite of his office as a subprior. Though the interpretations of an abbreviation he used to describe the room in another note are conflicting, he added the bemusing detail that his insight came while he was reading Paul's letter to the Romans in the tower latrine above the sewer. If so, it would have corroborated well what Luther would tirelessly emphasize: that the saving activity of God happened in mean and often filthy places. The birth of Jesus in a cow stall and his death among criminals were prime examples.

Luther's thinking at the time of this experience was strongly influenced by his study of the Psalms and the New Testament letters to the Galatians, Hebrews, and Romans. Now he focused on those two words that were focal in these: *righteousness* and *faith*. His teaching at this point is intricate and will sound unfamiliar, but it deserves careful attention because of its consequences. In respect to the first of these, in what Luther called His "alien" work, God exercised His "active" righteousness by punishing unrighteous humans. However, in His "proper" work God exercised "passive" righteousness in order to deal mercifully with them. Luther said that he had lived as a monk without reproach, but God's alien work and active righteousness left him with an extremely anguished conscience. Here came a truly upsetting self-disclosure: "I did not love, yes, I hated the righteous God who punishes sinners and secretly, if not blasphemously, certainly murmuring greatly, I was angry with God."

Night and day, he said, he then meditated on the word *righteousness* in one line from the apostle Paul's quotation of a verse from the prophets: "It is written, 'He who through faith is righteous shall live.'" Through the gift of faith believers received divine favor and liberation. In his own case, Luther wrote that he thereupon felt altogether born again and entered paradise through open gates. He now praised God, he added, "with a love as great as the hatred with which I had before hated the word 'righteousness of God.'"

Faith, therefore, was the other word in the same passage of Scripture that Luther pondered night and day: "The one who is righteous will live by faith." For years he had been taught that God would reward evil for evil and good for good. To experience interruption of that tit-for-tat idea, sinners needed the divine grace that they grasped in faith, which for him meant trust. He spoke of this turn as a free surrender and a joyful bet on what he named God's unfelt, untried, and unknown goodness. He concluded, "if your faith and trust are right, then your God is the true God." Faith and God always belonged together. Luther treated faith as something so potent that on occasion he almost made God seem like a product of human imagination. So he wrote: "as one believes, so one has," or "faith is the creator of the Deity, not in the substance of God, but in us." Faith is the creator of the Deity! The experience of divine love, not speculation about God, was at the heart of it all. "It is the nature of faith that it presumes on the grace of God." Therefore "faith does not require information, knowledge, or certainty." This from a struggler who remained passionate about finding certainty in faith throughout his life.

Coming down from his tower experience, Luther had to deal with the fact that he was on the run. With officials of empire and church in pursuit, he acted less like a hounded and cornered victim than like the wrestler engaged in open combat with God and humans, using his mouth and pen to defend himself and to counterattack. He had three major opportunities to do this in oral disputations. Two of these occurred in 1518 at Heidelberg and at the Diet of Augsburg, and the other at Leipzig in 1519.

Staupitz, aware of the furies in Luther's soul and the fires of response he was igniting, attempted to provide the monk with safe outlets. He appointed him to speak at the triennial chapter meeting of his order of Augustinian Hermits in Heidelberg. He sent Luther and a mandated companion on a 250-mile trip through dangerous territory to the meeting. For what it was worth, Frederick the Wise, stepping up further in his role as a protector, provided a letter assuring safe passage. Footsore and exhausted but ready for the encounter, Luther arrived in Heidelberg on April 18, 1518, to ready himself for debate in the philosophical faculty room at the university.

The atmosphere was not particularly unfriendly. At the crucial point in the encounter, bringing forth one of the more memorable images of his career, Luther claimed that the person who depended upon philosophical speculation in efforts to reach the "invisible" things of God dared not be called a theologian. He referred to the story in Exodus 33:23 where on Mount Sinai God permitted Moses no view of His face but only of His posterior. Luther boldly put it in Thesis 20: "The one who perceives the visible rearward parts of God as seen in suffering and the cross" deserves to be called a theologian. Talk about the hind end or back parts of God might sound offensive, but what Luther was here expounding would lead to his understanding of the theology of the cross over against what he called the theology of glory. The latter was his phrase for the argument of scholastic theologians who relied on Aristotle, defended indulgences, and thought humans could credibly seek merit from God through reason or good works.

The Heidelberg disputation was important also because it revealed Luther's persuasive power and the ability of the ideas nurtured at Wittenberg to find resonance elsewhere. After that April 26 event, the Dominican Martin Bucer, who was impressed enough to seek a privileged lunch with Luther and Staupitz, went home to promote change in the city of

Strasbourg. Bucer was to become an important figure on his own, as well as a moderate who could shuttle between the Wittenberg school and the developing evangelical movements around Huldreich Zwingli in Switzerland. Another convert to the cause was Johannes Brenz, who went on from Heidelberg to work for renewal in Württemberg, thus helping demonstrate that more was occurring than a revolt of the junior faculty at Wittenberg.

A non-Christian stumbling onto this scene might have understood Luther's resentment of an oppressive religious system but would have had great difficulty making sense of his reference to the cross of Jesus as being central to the most urgent human problem he knew, that of finding salvation. For all Christians, however, there could be no doubt that Luther was reaching to the core of their belief and addressing the foundation of their faith.

Rome responded by intensifying its pursuit of Luther. On August 7, 1518, he received a summons to an encounter that in the wrong setting could have led to his death. Never before or after did his situation look more ominous than now. However, since the elector and other protectors wanted to keep Luther close to home, Rome had to settle for a second-best though still dangerous site for the accused monk's appearance, an assembly called a diet in Augsburg. The papal legate who attacked him there was the foremost Dominican moralist, Jacobo di Vio de Gaeta, now Cardinal Cajetan.

The political situation helped Luther buy time. Well aware that Muslim forces were ready to attack Vienna and were threatening to besiege Europe, Cajetan was charged to get tax support for backing papal military operations. For strategic reasons, he was also to discourage electors from naming young Charles I of Spain the next emperor. Frederick the Wise and others from north of the Alps favored Charles, who could help them keep balance against papal power. When Cajetan made threats against Luther, Frederick in his civil role and Staupitz in his churchly situation both refused to be cowed. Staupitz released Luther from his Augustinian vows so that he would be free to travel and could speak out against the authority of the bishops, as a monk under discipline could not. Luther knew that Cardinal Cajetan was sent to pressure him to recant. Yes, he would appear at Augsburg. No, he would not recant. Word was going around that if he would not do so, he was to be bound in chains and taken to Rome.

A scornful Eck applied a new name to those in the growing company who criticized Rome. He called them Lutherans. Luther gave much better, or worse, than he got in response to that pejorative. Even five years later, in a tract on Psalm 120, Luther still included Eck among the "Mainz whoremongers and fat paunches," agents of the devil. In that document he rejected the Lutheran label, preferring the description evangelical, though later he was at ease with the description "evangelical or Lutheran." *Evangelical* signaled attachment to the evangel, the gospel, the promise of God, which is what the evangelicals claimed the Christians under papal obedience had long lost.

When the diet convened there was no way to avoid turning what was supposed to be a fatherly hearing into an irresolvable clash. During the three-day encounter at Augsburg, Cajetan, now the ablest defender of papal power, demonstrated that he and Luther lived in two different churchly worlds. "Who knows whether this is really true?" That older question by Luther now became a new challenge in the face of the papal claim for unique church authority. Luther was not answering "No one knows" but instead was charging "It is really *not* true." It was untruthful to claim on biblical grounds that one could find certainty in God's favor by keeping the divine law. It was false to claim that anything other than divine grace offered through the promise of God could rescue mortals or that the papacy could regulate the channels of grace.

At the end of his trip to the diet Cajetan had failed both to raise the revenues he had been sent to get and to ensnare Luther, whom he called "this beast" with the "deep-set eyes and strange ideas in his head." On the night of October 20, virtually defenseless against raw elements and would-be imprisoners, Luther stole away from Augsburg. A year to the day after he publicized his 95 Theses he had to find temporary refuge back in Wittenberg.

A fretting Cajetan tried to pressure Frederick to deliver the monk. Luther, not knowing the extent of Frederick's convictions and efforts and fearing that his prince was wavering, wrote him that rather than see the elector harmed he would be ready to leave his protection. The prince, who was not outspoken about his theological commitments and who never met Luther, acted again on his behalf, for political reasons but also no doubt because of his friendships with partisans of Luther's cause. Cautious and not given to self-disclosure, he did provide some indications that he identified with the emerging evangelical theology, even though it would challenge the market for and hence revenue from his collection of relics.

An explanatory letter arrived from the elector, a note that Luther read and reread because it helped assure him that, for now at least, he was likely to live. Frederick made clear that he would not surrender Luther, who had not been convicted of heresy. While in Saxony, Cajetan dared not issue the papal document he carried in condemnation of Luther, especially while he was still trying to prevent the election of the Saxon's favorite, King Charles I of Spain, as emperor.

On November 28 Luther decided on a new strategy. He issued an appeal for a general council of the church, an instrument that could in some ways serve to counter the pope. Some aides of Frederick the Wise who doubted that Luther could survive a trial advised, as if with hope against hope, that he should plead his case directly to Pope Leo X. Once more, local resentment against Rome and papal practices served Luther well. He uttered complaints that roused the locals and gave voice to their grievances. Thus he charged that "before long all the churches, palaces, walls and bridges of Rome will be built out of our money. First of all we should rear living temples, next local churches, and only last of all St. Peter's," which Saxons and their neighbors would never get to use. He went on, "Better that it should never be built than that our parochial churches should be despoiled." In such words he was reflecting the confidence he gained as he learned that much of the citizenry in the territories near him was now on his side. This did not mean, he added cautiously, that all Christians there should turn their backs on all that the church represented and was doing, but when it came to confronting the Roman power center he wanted to debate how to effect change.

The pious ruler Duke George of Saxony, called the Bearded, envied the growing power of his cousin Frederick the Wise and sneered at his toleration of the Wittenberg rebels. He thought that authorities could corner Luther in a debate at Leipzig, a city that he believed with good cause was largely unfriendly to the Wittenberger. Luther's foes grew optimistic about the potential outcome of such a disputation when they learned that the skilled debater Johannes Eck would represent them against the less capable representative of Wittenberg's cause, Luther's colleague Andreas Karlstadt.

Preparing for a hoped-for part in this third encounter with authorities, now scheduled in late June and early July of 1519, Luther brought focus and concreteness to his questioning. Once more a version of the question "Who knows whether this is really true?" framed his address to the content of specific papal utterances and some decisions of the church councils. The Western church of his time held as true the proposition that the pope ruled by divine right, so it was hazardous to challenge his churchly authority. Similarly, it was dangerous to contend that official church councils through the ages could have erred, but Luther began openly to do both.

In letters and treatises leading up to the debate, Luther, other Wittenberg theologians, and their growing company elsewhere came out in the open with clear charges: The pope rules by human authority. He is fallible. The periodically called church councils often contradicted one another and such councils at times erred grossly. As Luther knew, such charges were life-threatening to anyone who voiced them, because for Europeans to challenge popes and councils was to undercut authority, stability, certainty, and what was held to be God's truth in the church and the civil order alike.

Luther, the now open challenger, came to Leipzig not as a solitary individualist staking out a heroic claim for himself over against all of the church. For instance, he argued that the Eastern church, which he called Greek, was more orthodox and had produced better theologians than had Rome, yet it never submitted to papal authority. Still, he was ready to support the papacy as a human institution, seen as one agency among others of a social body, the community called church.

It was because Cajetan had worked to silence Luther after Augsburg and because presiding Duke George also did not want him to debate that Karlstadt, who had written theses in defense of Luther and attacking Eck, became the designated speaker. The audiences, however, were clearly waiting for Eck versus Luther on the subjects of papal authority and papal primacy, and Luther was eventually allowed to step up. The wily and capable Dominican scored points when he tried to tie Luther to the condemned heresy that had ended in the execution of Jan Hus of Bohemia a century before. It took many words and much skill for Luther to keep attacking Rome and yet not be simply identified with Hussitism, an identification that would likely have led to a death sentence.

Audiences wearied or drifted away as the debate wore down and ended inconclusively. Opinion about the outcome depended on the eye of the beholder. Most Leipzigers thought Eck had triumphed, while Wittenbergers deemed that, though scarred by some of Eck's sallies, Luther was the winner. In the aftermath, heresy hunters profited most. Eck wasted little time; he traveled to Rome in 1520 to appeal for officials to take action against the rebel. He knew that Rome would find good reasons to be angered. It was clear that Luther had now moved beyond mere criticism of the pope, whom he began to call the Antichrist, and was questioning not only some decrees of church councils but their authority itself. He was left with no authority but the Bible and no decisive answer to the question as to who should be its interpreter. Rome asked again, Should centuries of churchly teaching fall because of the personal experience of one monk?

Given the power of the pope and the bishops, the emperor and most princes, and especially an enraged Duke George of Saxony, it is tempting to picture a heroic Luther as utterly isolated. It does not take anything from the story of his conscience and courage, however, to point out that he was not entirely alone. He always had the protection of Frederick as well as Georg Spalatin, an assistant to Frederick and broker between the prince and Professor Luther. His message and cause were attracting ever more colleagues and friends from among people who also chafed under the twin oppressions of church and empire, believers whose spiritual strivings matched his and who were ready to share risks with him.

So far among them we have met only Karlstadt, a rather reckless Wittenberg Augustinian, who soon grew impatient with the pace Luther set and introduced so many innovations so rapidly—he was among the first of the priests in this company to marry, and he radically changed orders of worship—that he caused Luther trouble. The two eventually broke. But Luther found other friends. A gregarious sort who welcomed company, Luther attracted ordinary townspeople along with highly educated and strong-willed people in their own right. By far the most important of these was Philip Melanchthon, a prodigious linguist who came to teach classics and languages at Wittenberg in 1518 and who was at Luther's side at Leipzig. More cautious and more scholarly than Luther, he drafted some of the most important documents representing their cause and was on the scene at many decisive moments. The personalities of the two men differed vastly and they often came to misunderstandings. But Melanchthon complemented Luther and formulated their message in systematic ways while Luther stormed ahead, expressing himself more informally in sermons and tracts.

John Bugenhagen of Pomerania, who arrived in 1522 and became the city's pastor a year later, was converted to Luther's approach upon reading a tract by the Wittenberg professor at a dinner one evening. Best described as Luther's confessor and pastor, he also helped spread the cause to other cities and territories. Justus Jonas, another confidant, was also a humanist-trained professor who moved from Erfurt to the Castle Church in Wittenberg, also in 1522. Professor Nikolaus von Amsdorf was another to whom Luther turned at Wittenberg. Without this set of co-workers it is hard to picture even a risk-taking Luther surviving and keeping his focus.

While he was attracting these friends close to home, portentous events were occurring in the Holy Roman Empire, a loose federation of states more than a true empire. Frederick the Wise refused to serve after other electors showed preference for him as the next emperor, so the grandson of the recently deceased emperor Maximilian I, a nineteen-year-old Hapsburg brought up in Spain and the pope's least favored candidate, became Emperor Charles V. Said to address God in Latin, women in French, and his horse in German, he could not master the languages he needed to govern many of his subjects and was not well poised to interpret what was going on around him. The most powerful monarch in Europe for decades, he was destined to be the imperial antagonist and often frustrated hunter of Luther for the rest of his life.

Charles in pursuit would have had no trouble recognizing Luther, so familiar had he become and so abundant were word-portraits of him. Thus those who attended the debate at Leipzig would have seen something of what an admirer, Wittenberg rector Peter Mosellanus, dutifully recorded: "Martin is of medium height with a gaunt body that has been so exhausted by studies and worries that one can almost count the bones under his skin; yet he is manly and vigorous, with a high, clear voice." Also, "in his life and behavior he is very courteous and friendly, and there is nothing of the stern stoic or grumpy fellow about him." Adjustable, "in a social gathering he is gay, witty, lively, ever full of joy, always has a bright and happy face, no matter how seriously his adversaries threaten him." On the downside, Mosellanus in understatement found him "too violent and cutting in his reprimands."

Wittenberg student George Benedict also sketched this impression inside the cover of his Bible: Luther "was a man of medium size. His voice could be as sharp as it could be gentle, i.e., gentle in tone, sharp in the enunciation of syllables, words, and caesuras. He spoke with quick wit and expression in such logical fashion as if each thought flowed from the previous one." Benedict went on without embarrassment to claim: "Even the worst enemies of the gospel, having heard him only once, had to admit that on the basis of the surpassing significance of what they had heard, they had not been hearing a human being but the Holy Spirit speak; and that his remarkable doctrine therefore did not originate in him but was the working of a—good or demonic—spiritual power." Cajetan and Eck would, of course, have chosen demonic.

Such extreme views of the man came easily because he was himself a man of extremes. He did not favor middleground or gray areas but instead loved paradox and contradiction. The stormy contender was not the kind of person who could say to an opponent, "Perhaps you have a point." He had the courage to stare popes and emperors in the face, but even after his affirmation of faith, he often lived with dread. A man of passions given to verbal violence, he could also be tender, compassionate, and lyrical in his writings. A maker of enemies, he also attracted friends and loyalists. A man of the people, he was unawed by popes but often too awed by princes. Zealous for God, he developed a theology which honored the secular realms of life. Efforts to explain him by reference to his parents, his schooling, his radical decision to enter the monastery, or the eros that he displayed toward the search for God, the love of learning, and eventually the taking of a wife together do not finally provide simple reasons to explain why *this* monk, *this* biblical scholar, so upset his world and began to shape a new one.

An engraving by notable artist Lucas Cranach in 1520 shows Luther as a thirty-seven-year-old monk, cowled and tonsured, tense and unsmiling. His eyes look pinched, but it is not hard to see why they drew attention and attracted adjectives such as "piercing." The emperor or any papal posse assigned to track down this troublemaker could have used such a portrait on a Wanted poster. There was no question but that Luther, being chased, was wanted. He did not hold still and become a sitting target as he embarked in 1520 on a furious effort to define his understanding of the promise and the experience of God for a fast-changing Europe.

CHAPTER TWO

Defining the Life of Faith

1520–1525

IN 1513 POPE LEO X, a Florentine ruler from the Medici family, succeeded Pope Julius II, a fighter for the Papal States against France. A political and military more than a spiritual or theological figure, Leo was made a cardinal at age fourteen. Busy though he was warding off the continuing military threat of rival France and eager to buy votes for his favored candidate in an imperial election, he found time to become a humanist, a lover of the arts, someone remembered for a way of life that matched a phrase often attributed to him: "God has given us the papacy. Let us enjoy it." Leo took up the task of building on Julius' efforts to complete the great basilica above the presumed grave of St. Peter in Rome. Needing money for that edifice, he looked north of the Alps to territories about which he knew little in efforts to find much cash.

While cornering Luther was not the prime item on his papal agenda, Leo could not for long ignore the challenge and unrest inspired by the Augustinians at Wittenberg and their ever-growing circle of allies. Assigned to scrutinize Luther, cardinals and papal scholars found forty-one specific scandalous or unorthodox teachings in his writings. So on

June 15, 1520, a document called a bull, marked with Leo's red papal seal, went forth. In language that summoned God, Peter, Paul, the communion of saints, and the whole of the Christian church to action, the bull threatened Luther with excommunication. The document quoted the language of prayer from Psalm 74, a call for God to arise, in this case against the wild boar Martin Luther.

The idea for the metaphor may well have come when Leo and his riding partner Eck were hunting one day. In any case, the authors of the bull charged that a wild boar from the woods was threatening to destroy the vineyard that was the church. To Rome, Luther appeared ready to dig away at and destroy the church from the very roots up. Warming to the subject, the authors of the bull piled on metaphors, speaking of Luther's errors as a virus no longer to be tolerated and of him as a serpent creeping through the fields of the Lord. It was not hard to get the idea: The pope now wanted Frederick the Wise and other electors to track down Luther and his patrons, disciples, and supporters, male and female. They would collect a reward if they burned Luther's writings. They were to turn Luther over to Rome, where he could become a candidate for the flames.

In the fall of 1520 Eck returned from Rome to Frederick's Saxony to spread the word of condemnation. Another papal legate, the humanist Jerome Aleander, headed farther to Louvain and Amsterdam, where he succeeded in getting some books by Luther burned. Elsewhere north of the Alps, however, many of those in responsible positions greeted the zealots from Rome with cold, or at least shrugged, shoulders. More and more electors, princes, mayors, monks, scholars, and, of course, students aligned themselves with Luther's camp. They would not burn their cherished books or betray the dangerous rogue with whom they boldly identified. While he was in pursuit of Luther, Aleander complained that his delegation was outnumbered, since nine-tenths of the people in territories near Luther supported the monk passionately.

Though Luther saw himself as part of the official church, most of the time the rhetoric he employed against it was blustery, as evidenced in his reply to the papal pursuer in June 1520. He charged that everyone in Rome had become "mad, foolish, raging, insane, fools, sticks, stones, hell and evil." So he spit out: "Farewell, unhappy, hopeless, blasphemous Rome!" and continued, "The wrath of God come upon you, as you deserve." He went on to recall that he and his colleagues had cared for the Babylon that was Rome, but she was not healed. So they must leave her to become "the habitation of dragons, specters and witches and true to the name of Babel, an everlasting confusion, a new pantheon of wickedness."

Over against such outbursts, Luther the theologian also found it important to say that though the faith and practices of Rome were often corrupt, so long as the papists properly baptized, they remained part of the Body of Christ. As for the other sacrament that would prove to be his major point of contention with Rome, the Mass, or the Lord's Supper, while he complained that Rome violated Christ's mandate by offering bread but not wine, still it remained truly a sacrament. For all its rough character, there was therefore some nuance in his stance. He did not share the claim of some radical colleagues that they were overleaping fifteen centuries to restore an original pure church. Luther was aware that there had been faintheartedness and corruption in even the earliest apostolic church. Positively, he saw the church in Wittenberg or Rome or anywhere in biblical terms as the place where God dwells, thriving among the people God loves, having as its purpose bringing people to the kingdom of heaven, because the church was heaven's gate.

As pressure on Luther increased, those monks who chose to associate with him took risks. Rome knew that when he attacked canon law, the legal formulations of the church that were a foundation of so much of European life, Luther was disobeying the church as well as its secular counterpart, the civil authority that enforced ecclesiastical edicts. Officials could seize him in the name of church and empire and put him to death. Friends and enemies alike were puzzled to see how Luther could be as productive as he was in the face of such threats and hazards. He produced important theological works at a furious pace while, in effect, leading a movement and making practical decisions.

Often, to spread news or draw wider support, a town crier or a preacher acting as one would read a new tract to Luther's public, whose growing numbers expected ever more excitement. So it was that many Wittenbergers awoke on the morning of December 10, 1520, to witness an event scheduled at the gate that opened on the city dump. There,

in a wildly ironic defense of academic freedom, students in-
cinerated anti-Luther writings. Luther himself did the really
dangerous thing when he thereupon burned books of canon
law. Almost incidentally, it would appear, that while trembling he also tossed into the flames a copy of the papal threat
of his excommunication. Philip Melanchthon heard him
charge that because the pope had confounded God's truth, it
was not Luther but God who that day was confounding and
condemning the pope to the fire.

Observing the fateful day at the Wittenberg gate inspires
reflection as to where Luther's act left him in the face of the
church. Even more than before, he kept producing texts in
which he contended that people who joined him in his
protest should and did remain members of the Christian
community. He who is to find Christ, he wrote, must first
find the churches. Luther preferred to call the church the
communion of saints, and in the Latin version of the Apostles' Creed he used *Christian* instead of the word *catholic*.

He contended that no one can build his own bridge to
heaven. Faith and community were of a piece in the church,
which was not to him a vague philosophical ideal but a gathering of people connected to Christ. If they were now no
longer to be defined as the company of believers who were
under papal obedience, he had to describe how they related
to each other and to Christ: Through one faith, he said, they
adhered to Christ and appeared as one body with Him and
He with them. Christ was the Head and they were the members. The sacraments, Luther thought, helped make this

church real, but only God knew who were truly members in faith. The new believer was drawn to saving faith through the believing community and nurtured at the bosom of the church as mother. There was no mention of separate sects or church bodies.

Between the threat of excommunication in the summer of 1520 and the burning of the bull by Luther that December, the professor, preacher, and pamphleteer of Wittenberg was also at his desk, writing at least three classic publications: *Address to the Christian Nobility of the German Nation*, *The Babylonian Captivity of the Church*, and *The Freedom of a Christian*. These further developed the cases that gave Rome good reason to condemn their author and provided the critics of Rome clear reasons to rally around him. While one cannot easily measure exactly what the various readers took from the booklets and the cartoons in them, it was clear that what was happening in Wittenberg was causing tumult and that it inspired Luther to treat the moment with a mixture of fear and zest.

Luther never became a formal systematic theologian. Most of his writings addressed practical situations. Thus his populist *Address to the Christian Nobility* opened with its author professing humility and calling himself a fool. He appealed to the local nobles to join the attack on Rome and call a church council on their own to oppose the selling of indulgences. Luther therewith further indicated that he was giving up on efforts to communicate with church authority and that he was audaciously going directly to the public through the princes.

The *Address* did not call for abolition of the papacy. Luther raged instead against papal malpractice and the pope's extravagant claims to temporal power. He had been reading new documentary evidence that exposed old forgeries on the basis of which the pope claimed dominion. Luther went on with the radical claim that priestly and papal offices should not be based on decree or designed to promote the higher status of some Christians. Startling in its novelty and boldness was his definition of the priesthood of all believers. This appealing theme had less to do with governance than with new understandings of baptism and prayer, but these were revolutionary. In the world that Christians were trained to think of in hierarchical terms, this booklet declared that *all* the baptized were now worthy equally to stand before God, forgiving and praying for others without priestly mediation. Luther was here concerned less with the exercise of authority in this broad priesthood than with the license for all people to represent all interests in prayer. In fact, fearing chaos and preferring order, Luther did not set out to eliminate ordained priests and bishops. He recognized their offices and assignments; they simply were not to remain a superior class that held unique powers and sanctions. They were deputies or vicars for the whole body of believers as they carried on pastoral tasks.

After having set out to find ways to supplant the power of the pope and priests of the old order, Luther in October next attacked the sacramental system in a Latin booklet aimed at clergy and scholars, *The Babylonian Captivity of the Church*. It was only the beginning of an onslaught, but it provided plenty of evidence that Rome knew what it was doing when it condemned Luther. Developing the biblical metaphor in its title, this publication claimed that as God's ancient people had been exiled in Babylon, now the pope, the self-styled Vicar of Christ, had led believers into a new captivity. With this Antichrist active, Luther deduced and proclaimed that the end of history and the last judgment must be near.

While coming to the points chiefly at issue between himself and Rome, Luther used the word *sacrament*, though he did not like it. He generally affirmed the current form of baptism, though he found fault with the way he thought priests sometimes turned it into something like magic when they made too little of faith that came with the Word of God in connection with baptismal water. Through baptism the Holy Spirit simply turned sinners into servants of God and members of the priesthood of all believers.

The other sacrament that he would keep, the Lord's Supper, raised more troubling issues and received more notice. The Lord's Supper had become a weapon with which the hierarchy could keep rulers and people in line. Without forgiveness of sins assured in the Mass, sinners were in danger of suffering eternal hellfire. Luther retained everything that did not get in the way of the grace of the sacrament, so his whole focus was on the Word that was connected with the elements of bread and wine. Centrally, this included Jesus' command to "do this," meaning "do" receive bread and wine as the body and blood of Christ, in remembrance of him and to believe his promise that forgiveness of sins came with faith in the words that produced this sacrament.

For Luther the drastic change came in the understanding of the central words of the Mass. As he observed it, through the words and actions of the canon of the Mass, the church through the centuries had gradually turned the rite into an offering, a sacrifice by the priest and people. But if ordinary humans, even those ordained as priests, could actually make a sacrifice, the gift of Christ's death and its benefits were rendered unnecessary and even pointless, in Luther's eyes. Instead, the church must reject sacrifice because it represented human work and thus stood in the way of grace. The sacrament was God's gift, not an impetus for human striving and a claim on God.

To ease the transition in worship, he proposed some revised forms, a Latin Formula for the Mass and a German Mass. Framing all this was the New Testament story of how the night before he was killed Jesus hosted a Last Supper with disciples and commanded them to keep gathering often for such a meal in remembrance of him. The Antichrist, he thought, in his papal assault on faith, had corrupted this meal in three limiting ways. First, people received only bread, not wine. Second, using philosophy to explain the rite, the papacy treated the bread and wine as being changed in substance into the body and blood of Jesus. Luther argued with some intricacy that in this mystery Christ was singularly but not magically present. Unless the words with which Christ instituted the Lord's Supper were spoken, the bread and wine remained mere bread and wine. Third, by turning the sacrament into a sacrifice and setting up regulations and rules about it, the pope had found in the Mass a political and of course an economic instrument with which to subdue those hungry for salvation. People thought they could merit God's favor by participating.

The booklet on the Babylonian Captivity also treated other sacraments in the Roman church. Luther did support a version of penance and sometimes even called it a sacrament, but he continued his lifelong crusade against what he regarded as its misuses. As to the first of the remaining four sacraments, while the New Testament Letter of James had urged ministering to the gravely ill with the use of anointing oil and prayer, Luther saw the current version of the rite to be corruptible, one more means by which the manipulative church held people in bondage. Next, he thought that confirmation may be a valuable act but it did not convey grace and there was no biblical command to institute it. Third, ordination to priesthood was no sacrament, since all baptized believers were already priests. They should elect and approve some to minister among them but should not elevate these to a new caste or assign them high status.

Finally, God did not impart grace through marriage, so it also was not a sacrament. But it was holy. Luther at first praised marriage when he would downgrade celibacy, but now he began to stress its positive good and said he wanted all who could marry to do so. In his teaching and evangelical practice the former sacrament of marriage became a civil rite blessed by the church. "Matrimony is outside church business," he wrote, since it was "a governmental concern, hence up to the magistracy." He attacked Rome for commercializing marriage by means of its laws and argued in crude language that the church had become a merchant selling vulvas, genitals, and pudenda of both sexes. Though marriage was not a sacrament, on biblical grounds he argued that divorce could occur only if a spouse committed adultery, deserted the other, or, in some cases, was impotent. Unless adultery or desertion was proven in particular cases, divorce was worse than bigamy.

Treatises like the one on Babylonian Captivity provoked more counterattacks. Some of Luther's friends thought that to protect himself he should show the pope that there was nothing personal in all this. He responded with a letter that mingled fawning praise for the papal office with some sympathy for the pope. Now for a moment he chose to see the pope as a lamb among wolves, a man who was surrounded by monsters who deserved his slashing critiques. It is not likely that the pope ever read the letter, but in any case he would not have been appeased. Read on, Luther urged his blessed father Leo. Attached was *The Freedom of a Christian,* a "little treatise dedicated to you as a token of peace and good hope." Dashed off in German and rewritten in Latin, in the eyes of many it became a classic document of liberation.

Right off, Luther proposed two theses that, he admitted, seemed to cancel each other: "A Christian is a perfectly free lord of all, subject to none. A Christian is a perfectly dutiful servant of all, subject to all." The lines capture what was central to Luther and demonstrate how sharply he could pose two such seeming contradictions against each other and then make sense of them for believers. To support the theses he drew on conjugal, almost erotic images from the apostle Paul.

Thus one benefit of faith, he wrote, was that it united the soul with Christ as a bride is united with her bridegroom. Paul had written that Christ and the soul became "one flesh," more or less as married couples do, but this was a perfect marriage. The soul and Christ in common share both good *and* evil. Contrast made this unity vivid: "Christ is full of grace, life, and salvation. The soul is full of sins, death, and damnation." Faith comes between Christ and the soul, so that an exchange results. The soul henceforth will own what is Christ's and Christ must suffer what belongs to the soul. If Christ gives the soul "his body and very self," Luther asked, "how shall he not give her all that is his? And if he takes the body of the bride, how shall he not take all that is hers?"

Luther admitted what any reader might surmise, that this view of grace was hard to grasp but, understand it or not, he knew that every believer experienced it. He continued to employ marital language and metaphor: "Here this rich and divine bridegroom Christ marries this poor, wicked harlot," the believing self, and then "adorns her with all his goodness." In the biblical script that Luther provided, the soul could say with the Song of Solomon: "My beloved is mine and I am his." This exchange, he argued, is to be rooted in nothing but faith, not in human striving and achievement. Luther trumpeted his line that the Christian is a "perfectly free lord of all, subject to none," thanks to the joyful exchange with Christ.

He used different colorings to shade the important concept of the exchange, depending upon the variety of contexts, and so do translators of the German adjective *fröhlich*. I have collected some of them, having found the concept so central and communicable: Alongside "joyful," we read that the exchange is "happy," "fortunate," "cheerful," "glorious," or "blessed." In every case, "What Christ has is the property of the believing soul, what the soul has becomes the property of Christ." The sinner brings sin; the righteous Christ brings righteousness. In this exchange Christ changes places with sinners, something that Luther agreed the heart can grasp only in faith. Luther inherited, was at ease with, and even enlarged on some other biblical metaphors for the way God and humans were brought together in Christ, but they do not convey the sense of certainty that the concept of the joyful exchange so dramatically did.

At the same time, in the second part of the thesis, the Christian is servant of all, subject to all. Having sounded so assured, even reckless, about the perfection that related to the subject of faith, Luther now had to rescue the works of love. Otherwise believers, he feared, would find more reason to remain lawless, whorish, captive of sins, death, and damnation. Luther had fought against the notion of finding certainty in relation to God by striving, by being obsessive about the works of the divine law. So now he simply stressed the human identification with God as being like bridal love; faith was to be active in love. Here again was the root of Luther's evangelical ethic. Being busy trying to do good works could obscure the promises of God. Becoming aware of the failure to please God would leave sinners in despair. But following the law of God now became part of the free believer's expression of faith.

The pope had other business on his mind than reading booklets like these three. Although Luther had burned the bull as well as the bridges behind him in the summer of 1520, he had still not been officially put out of the pope's church. Another bull announced his excommunication on January 3, 1521. This most severe theological judgment was at the very least humiliating and inconveniencing. Unlike clergy in good standing, those excommunicated had to pay taxes, serve in the military, and ordinarily lose housing and subsidy. At worst, excommunication could lead to death, and Luther was a worst case. On January 18 the pope followed up with orders to the new emperor, now titled Charles V, to carry out the ban. Would he? Could he? The political situation and the now immense popularity of the wild boar still frustrated him because it prevented such action.

While Luther, as the faith-full bride of Christ, felt assured in relation to God, in human affairs he felt unsure and had good reason to do so. If the pope could not let the wild boar tear up the vineyard, the emperor must track down the monkish beast in a task he did not relish but that he had to believe was valid. If there was to be a trial for an apprehended Luther, Frederick the Wise wanted it to take place in a court located safely close to home. His case therefore became an agenda item at a forthcoming diet, an imperial assembly of estates, to be convened at Worms in April 1521. Jerome Aleander and other papal representatives were glad to follow through with plans for it. In that region Charles V had no choice but to ensure safe conduct to Luther, whose only announced options would be to recant or not to recant.

Although urged by friends not to risk martyrdom by appearing, Luther obeyed the summons issued on March 6, 1521. Though understandably fearful, he invoked the divine presence to help him put on at least a mask of courage. After a friend supplied a covered wagon he rode to Worms, being greeted in town after town as a conquering and unconquerable hero. To the great disgust of imperial and papal officials, people trumpeted and cheered his entry into the cathedral city.

Chambers of commerce knew how to exploit events like the diet and turn them also to popular and profane purposes. Contemporary reports suggest that some visitors were up in arms, others down in their cups, drinking, or about town in the embraces of prostitutes. Within the chamber of the trial, however, all was serious. Luther's moment on the stand came when on April 17 he was asked: Were all these stacked books his? *Could* that many be his? Luther examined the piles. Yes, they were all his.

He startled and confused his followers and the larger audience with his next act. He asked for time to consider his situation and was given until the next day to recant. Supporters could only speculate why such a prepared man suddenly delayed. To find his voice? To ponder one last time whether he was sure that he dared go against the developed teaching of the church? So he could once more consult his own books or to devise a strategy that might save his neck and his growing movement? No one knows.

In the candlelight of the next evening he calmly stood his ground. Asked one more time simply to recant all he had written in the books, he replied that he could not do this categorically, because the writings fell into several groups. It would have been trivial for him to recant some of them, he said, since they dealt with peripheral matters. At the opposite extreme, for him to recant those that expressed the truth of God in congruence with the Word of God would damage his soul, the church, and the empire.

He then made history with his most remembered words: "Since then your serene majesty and your lordships seek a simple answer, I will give it in this manner, neither horned nor toothed. Unless I am convinced by the testimony of the Scriptures or by clear reason (for I do not trust either in the Pope or in the councils alone, since it is well known that they have often erred and contradicted themselves), I am bound by the Scriptures I have quoted and my conscience is captive to the Word of God. I cannot and I will not retract anything, since it is neither safe nor right to go against conscience." Some reports have him adding, "I cannot do otherwise, here I stand," and then, "May God help me. Amen." In the chaos that followed, as the emperor gave up on the proceedings, some heard Luther shout, "I am finished." The papal legate Aleander reported that this gesture matched that of German mercenaries when they rejoiced over a strong blow in their tournaments. He drafted a condemnatory Edict of Worms, but Charles was not in a position to sign it for political reasons.

The emperor complained that a single monk, beguiled by his own private judgment, had chosen to stand by himself against the faith that he believed all Christians had held for a thousand years. Even worse was Luther's added charge that the popes and the councils had erred. So Charles resolved to follow through against him, saying that he was ready to stake upon this cause all his dominions, his friends, his body and his blood, his life, and his soul. His not yet signed edict called on all the emperor's kingdoms, territories, friends, body and blood, life and soul to stand against Luther. After Mass on May 26 he finally did sign the document, in effect making Luther an unprotected outlaw, at the mercy of everyone.

While anyone who gave Luther refuge could be in jeopardy with him, the grudging emperor still had to keep his own pledge of safe conduct for Luther's return from Worms. Though condemned by pope and emperor alike, Luther could momentarily let his guard down. He stopped at Moehra to visit his grandmother and to preach. Farther on the way home toward Wittenberg he again attracted crowds and held the pulpit in other town churches. With the protecting princes and clamoring townspeople gathered in safe sanctuaries, he should have enjoyed a moment of simple triumph. The nervous priests who provided pulpits, however, knew as Luther did that there was no reason for them to breathe easily. The safe-conduct pledge would soon expire, after which citizens were supposed to track the errant monk and bring him to justice.

Backstage, officials uneasy about harboring Luther in public still schemed to save his neck while protecting their own. A dramatic scheme unfolded on May 4. Toward Altenstein, in the very Thuringian forest wilds where he had picked berries as a child, a band of horsemen swooped down to the road, drawn crossbows in hand. Luther's friend Nikolaus von Amsdorf, at his side, went through the motions of resisting them. While he had been privy to a specific strategy, Luther had only at best been aware of a vague and general notion that he might be seized and taken to a safe haven. The horsemen scooped up Luther, blindfolded him, and took him to the largely abandoned Wartburg Castle near Eisenach.

In that stronghold his captors ordered the monk to seclude himself in two rooms, to trade his monk's robe for knightly gear, to let his beard grow, and to let a head of hair replace his tonsure. They described this curious new visiting noble as Junker Georg, Knight George. Let uninformed Wittenberg mourn his disappearance; Luther was temporarily safe. Eloquent testimony to the sense of void that his absence would mean to humanistic supporters came from Nuremberg artist Albrecht Dürer's diary. He noted in it that Luther "had treacherously been taken captive" by ten horsemen who "perfidiously led away this betrayed and devout man." Had he been murdered? Would those he had led to the truth now return to the influence of false teachers of blind doctrine? The artist concluded: "O God, to think of what he might have been able to write for us in another ten or twenty years!"

Dürer need not have worried. Luther wrote more in his ten months cooped up in the castle than most scholars could write in ten years. He did not only write. He also enjoyed birdsongs, sights of nature, and the open skies, while he found himself, as he said, drunk with leisure. In confinement, he experienced characteristic mood swings that sometimes led him to the depths of depression. Like the Jacob about whom he later wrote, he again struggled with himself and with God. When his friend Philip Melanchthon wrote a letter in which he praised him for his faith, Luther ruefully responded that the troubles of his soul had not yet ceased and that his previous weakness of faith still persisted.

The confident view his friend held only added to his torment. He wrote of his confinement, "I sit here like a fool and, hardened in leisure, pray little, do not sigh for the Church of God." Burning not in the spirit but in the body, as he put it, he made an inventory of his ailments that included his always troubling and sometimes traumatic bouts with constipation and hemorrhoids, to which he referred with tiring regularity and some crudeness. Never was he more vulnerable to depression, he wrote, than when he would lie awake in the castle chamber, blaming the devil. At a crisis moment Luther wrote to his friends on July 13 that in the silence and loneliness of night in this idle solitude, he faced a thousand battles with Satan. Still, he suggested, contending with that spiritual devil was easier than fighting some humans.

For all the setbacks and frustrations he experienced during these months, Junker Georg plunged forward with a flood of letters and other writings that signaled to the people down the hill that Luther was alive and full of fighting spirit. The variety of subjects that he addressed dazzles. For example, he completed a tender devotional piece on the Magnificat, Mary's song in the Gospel of Luke, evidence of the fact that he remained devoted to the mother of Jesus.

If the tracts and booklets of these years served to define the life of faith, none of them did so much for the cause as his translation of the Bible, which he began at the Wartburg Castle. In the midst of the confusion during his fake kidnapping he had somehow managed to rescue and bring along his Bible, and he lived most intimately with it during his exile. Having dismissed hierarchy and pope, he and those with him had to find their authority in the Word of God as witnessed to in the Hebrew Scriptures, or the Old Testament, and in the Greek New Testament. He first turned the New Testament into the vernacular.

Skilled in the use of language and possessed of a good ear for dialect, Luther was poised to make the ancient gospels and epistles sound like the conversation of villagers in narratives cast in the equivalent of newspaper prose. To translate, write, and speak in the vernacular was one of the most radical and revolutionary choices he made. In fact, the vulgar, gross, and even grotesque barnyard and bathhouse expressions so regular in his work appear to be part of a strategy designed to give voice to and attract the common people who were so often excluded by elites in society and church.

As he set to work on the Bible, he found little help from existing translations, which were crude and inaccurate. Instead, he profited from a five-year-old critical edition of the Greek New Testament by Desiderius Erasmus of Rotterdam, the most influential humanist scholar of the day. In eleven weeks Luther produced a version that was published without his name in September 1522, to the profit of plundering publishers and awakened publics. Along with the Old Testament translation that appeared some years later, this Bible did more than any other book to begin to shape the modern German literary styles after having served also as a model for Luther's contemporaries.

Junker Georg strove to be extremely accurate but, being also Luther, he could not resist twisting his translation to match throughout what he found central in the letters of Paul. Thus he turned the blighted word *penance* into the German word for the "penitence" that he had evoked in his 95 Theses. When translating Paul's words about being saved by grace, Luther twice sneaked in the word *alone*, as in "by grace alone," to reinforce his attack on human works as instruments for pleasing God. So it is not surprising that critics found much to pick apart. One Jerome Emser wrote that he found fourteen hundred mistranslations in Luther's work, which he otherwise thought graceful and sweet and, hence, dangerous. In 1522 Emser came up with an alternative and more literal translation. Backed by Duke George, it sold reasonably well, but it was no competitor for Luther's.

In a subsequent battle over translation, Luther made a comment that threw special light on the Wartburg effort. It appeared later when he was contending with a Swiss scholar of Hebrew, Sebastian Münser. He reached into autobiography to make a point. Münser the scholar, he wrote, had missed much because he stood apart from the experiences that the biblical witness evoked. "Yes, dear Münser, you have never experienced these *Anfechtungen*," he chided. "But I sat with Jonah in the whale where everything seemed to be despair." There in the depths he also learned and experienced grace.

Junker Georg was still a monk, but he chafed in the face of monastic vows and now saw a need to counter the practices associated with them, for the sake of the church and souls. So from Wartburg in 1521 he issued *The Judgment on Monastic Vows*. It holds interest because Luther chose that moment to reflect on his troubling relation to his father back when the son entered the monastery. A remark to his friend Melanchthon as he prepared the treatise is revealing since it cuts to the marrow of Luther's personal uncertainties and doubts. In it he remembered that his earthly father had been angry over his monastic choice, and he elaborated on his emotional state.

Still rankling was the father's comment about that decision: "Let's hope that this was not a delusion from Satan." Hans had succeeded in planting or nurturing a doubt that was still nagging. Luther recalled that decisive encounter.

Nothing the father had ever said went deeper, Luther admitted, than when he did what Luther was so often to do, that is, quote Scripture. Hans asked, "Have you not also heard" that "parents are to be obeyed?" Then followed a profound and revealing confession. Luther pondered the effect of this jab by his father: "The word took such deep root in my heart that I have never heard anything from his mouth which came back to my mind more persistently." That phrase suggests that other parental words must also have haunted him. "It seemed to me," he wrote, "as if God had spoken to me from afar, through my father's mouth."

The preface attached to Luther's text on monasticism was a letter to that father. He wanted to tell, he wrote, what took place between the two sixteen years earlier when he had taken the vow to become a monk without his father's knowledge and against his will. The son was now tender as he specified concerns about his youthful inability to think clearly. "In your fatherly love you were worried about my weakness," he remembered, as well as about the son's unwillingness to be tied down with an honorable and profitable marriage. A reader might almost feel the shudders as Luther went on: "This fear of yours, this care, this indication against me was for a time implacable."

As for marriage, though by 1521, when the first priests began to wed, and 1523, when monks and nuns left their monasteries in considerable numbers—thirteen departed from Wittenberg that year—Luther remained celibate even though he no longer believed in the vows. He urged his father to be tolerant about his decision to remain so. Yes, he agreed, parents had their appropriate authority, but since Christ possessed more, he argued that his father had had to give in to the vocational choice of the son. Martin thereupon wrapped all human authorities into one package, one line, and rejected them all. Christ alone now, he wrote, was his immediate bishop, abbot, prior, lord, father, and teacher. If this Christ had thus taken one son away, many other sons of fathers, Luther argued, would be saved through his work so long as he remained in the ministry of the Word.

In the tract itself he argued that law—canon law, church law—should not keep people in the monastery. Those who chose to stay there dared not think of themselves as better than anyone else. Vows were good works of a sort that had no standing. His word on this subject questioned and blasted the foundation of European order. As they read of or heard such detonations and became convinced by them, monks and nuns began to escape the monasteries in numbers and on a scale unthinkable a few years earlier.

The idea of being released from vows fit well with what Luther had written on Christian freedom. No canon law, no earthly arrangements, dared stifle the human impulse to be free. Now he charged that the choice to undertake the vows was not a neutral matter; the vows were even *against* faith. It was a drastic move for him to assert that the only vow which mattered came not from humans but from God: God makes a vow to us, he wrote, to believers, in baptism. Also, as monks left their cells and then married, Luther noted, they were taking on a different kind of vow, but one that this God had explicitly intended and blessed.

Other documents from his seasons at the Wartburg Castle displayed Luther further defining his thought. In 1521 he replied to Latomus, a Louvain monk and inquisitor, who cited biblical texts against him. Latomus asked Luther whether as he attacked the tradition of the church in his day he should be so sure of himself. Could that church and its whole tradition be wrong? Was its authority not to be obeyed? Luther responded with a fury that may well have served as a disguise to cover his own enduring uncertainty.

"Every good work is sin," Luther responded. This sounded not only curious but offensive. Certainly everyone knew that a good work was a good work and as such it should please God. But Luther argued that if a good work was designed to attract God's favor and reward, it must fail and even be evil. He cited a metaphor from Isaiah, one that compared human righteousnesses to bloody menstrual cloths. This was twisting a gross image to fit Luther's understanding of human nature as he read of it in Paul's New Testament writings; it would become a key to all of his subsequent theology.

However, he went on, those who clung to the good news which came to them as a story and offered a promise became certain that Christ was for them. If such a theme seemed to glorify the human being who was "in Christ," then let it, Luther shrugged. He diagnosed the ailing heart: distress and anxiety in it simply led one to be all the more eager for joy. So when God made one just, he observed, the sinner became certain. This did not mean that anyone, and especially not Luther, would henceforth be free from all doubt or from mental trauma. No one going through the sea of life, he thought, could totally evade uncertainty any more than could those on long voyages at sea. Like Jacob, he would keep on wrestling. But the doubt, he contended, was itself a stirring up by the Christ who drove a person to make an appeal to him. So in Luther's writing, Christ says, "I am more certain to you than your own heart and conscience." And, he added, "Christ came into this world to make us most certain."

In each of his writings on this subject, Luther defined the life of faith more emphatically than before. Christ offered and *was* the promise, the gift of God, the grace that brought the believer into the scope of divine favor. A momentous formula for Luther's understanding came out of this claim, one that again displayed his love of paradox: The human is at the same time one who is made right with God *and* someone who sins. That concept distinguished Luther's thought not only from that of those who taught that works, along with grace, would bring one to God's favor. It also confused and confounded many others who were by now disaffected with the church of the day but were not ready to attack good works. He was to spend much of his energy during the rest of his career elaborating on this complex view of human nature and divine grace.

Where, critics asked, did that leave sinners as they dealt with the divine law? Luther had to deal with all the biblical passages that spoke of its power. Law, for him, both demonstrated and *was* the will of the holy God expressed against those who wanted to be perfect and to save themselves. In that context the divine law revealed how everyone fell short, how good works were not only not good but even worked against the aspiring believer who relied on them. Law produced knowledge of shortcomings or sin and left the believer bereft. When the sinner wanted to be right with God, there could be no appeal to the works of the divine law. In the matter of being declared just, the law of God always and only accused sinners, which meant it judged everyone in the church. Outside of that context, in the sphere of human interaction, the law was the message of God that related to the care of the neighbor and the good of society.

Sometimes the walls of Wartburg limited Luther's attempts to define the faith as he understood it. Restricted by them, he had difficulty facing challenges that came not only from Rome but also now from places like Wittenberg itself and from former allies who were moving on to radical paths. Thus his professorial colleague the impetuous Andreas Karlstadt, who had failed to hold the audience in the Leipzig debate but who did hold the strategic pulpit in the Castle Church, was pushing for drastic and sudden upheavals in the externals of church life.

Change therefore came where townspeople would perceive it most directly, in worship. On Christmas Day in 1521, Karlstadt broke precedent by shedding his priestly vestments. At the Lord's Supper he offered the laity both bread and wine and told them they sinned if they did *not* take the bread and the cup into their own hands before ingesting. He also scandalized many after he abandoned monastic life and married a sixteen-year-old country girl. Luther in theory should have approved the marriage, but Karlstadt and his following were so flamboyant and abrasive that he feared backlash.

Worse, in Martin Luther's eyes, student demonstrators, whom townspeople described as young and unruly "Martinians," not "Lutherans," in early December began threatening the health and safety of those they opposed. They smashed church windows, shattered sacred statues, and wielded knives as they demonstrated in the streets. With good reason the town council, observing the violence, expressed fear of full-scale riots. If anarchy and chaos prevailed, there was concern that these could lead to the demise of efforts at effecting positive changes in church and city.

In the face of these turbulences, in early December Luther temporarily left Wartburg to sneak into Wittenberg, where news of his presence soon became public. For diplomatic reasons he chose to be moderate in his response, though what he saw was disconcerting. He was anything but mild, however, when more radical partisans invaded the town. On December 27, three agitators, dubbed prophets from the town of Zwickau, came to disrupt the peace. He called them fanatics or enthusiasts, which meant that they claimed they were possessed by God as they advertised direct and immediate revelation. Though Luther was friendly to spiritual experience, the Zwickau prophets, he thought, went far beyond the boundaries set in the Bible.

Zwickau, a place known for its weaving industry, numbered about eight thousand souls. The gap between the haves and have-nots there had made the town noteworthy for its prosperity but also left it in danger of violence because of unrest across class lines. Thomas Müntzer, like Karlstadt a man once fanatically devoted to Luther, fired up the aggrieved. Luther saw his own relatively conservative teaching on the sacraments undercut by extremists. People who, he charged, listened to neither the Bible nor reason threatened all his work, since their excesses were contributing to the now regionwide fear that bloodshed was imminent. The Zwickau prophets and others like them were to haunt Luther for years, and he often turned in rage on their movement.

With Luther back at Wartburg after his brief visit, the Wittenberg town council met radical assaults less by repression than by adjusting to changed circumstances. In early 1522 the council came up with a far-reaching approach to social ills and other discontents by channeling alms and donations for the poor through a common chest. This practice made possible a kind of welfare program that assisted the unemployed, the poor, and those in need of education, while on the moral cleanup front the councillors closed the brothels. Crossing the line from town affairs to church life, they instituted forms of worship that reflected some of what both Karlstadt and the more cautious Luther desired. Karlstadt, however, was not tamed by these moves.

Alarmed by fears that the prince would tolerate none of this, disturbed by the hesitancy of his young lieutenant Philip Melanchthon to be a leader, and concerned about the fate of the gospel there, Luther returned to Wittenberg on March 6, 1522. He mounted the pulpit at the town church and for eight days preached sermons that further defined the evangelical movement and its central activity. We learn much about what Luther thought of preaching at this time from another document he wrote in Wartburg, titled *The Eight Wittenberg Sermons*. An edition of sermons in German, it displayed the professor self-cast in the role of preacher. He took pains to find the best printer for his sermons, since only from the page could he reach congregations away from the castle. He called *The Eight Wittenberg Sermons* his best book.

As he defined his thoughts on preaching, a consistent view emerged. The church was a mouth-house for speaking and not a pen-house for writing. In a German pun he insisted that the Word of God should be shouted more than written, so he shouted, or purred, when he preached, as the case and subject matter demanded. He could at one moment praise the townspeople in the congregation for their faithfulness and then in the next berate them for being besotted, stupid, and unready to put their faith to work in acts of love. He aimed right off at the hearts of listeners. His very first words in the published collection reveal something of the uncertainty he felt now that he was under threat of death, and he would share that feeling: "The summons of death comes to us all, and no one can die for another. Everyone must fight his own battle with death by himself." He also had to project confidence in these messages, and this he did.

The collection demonstrated how, after grounding his preached words in biblical texts, he commented on anything that struck him as relevant in the surrounding world. When pointing out how hard it was to preach with reference to the whole world, in one rare instance he even mentioned America, of which Europeans were then becoming aware. Reaching the souls of the congregation at Wittenberg often appeared to be more than enough for him as he saw the Day of Judgment nearing.

He also defined scriptural authority in the 1520s. It was urgent that he do this since, having repudiated official churchly authority, he and his associates were left with the Bible alone as the source and norm of their teaching. Not relying on scholastic doctrines that were traditionally used to prove the truth of the Scripture, he improvised his way into the thickets of biblical interpretation and led others to identify with this way. The Scripture, he said, was the womb from which were born theological truth and the church. The Scripture was an infallible guide to salvation, even though, contra the views of the scholastics, in his understanding its writers could and did make mistakes when writing on earthly matters.

Luther therefore saw no challenge to the authority and trustworthiness of the Bible when he caught a gospel writer assigning a quotation in the New Testament to the wrong Old Testament prophet or saw his favorite writer Paul the apostle producing a failed allegory. When he confronted a dark passage in the Bible, he said he found a bright or clear one to compensate for or illuminate the obscure teaching. While the Old Testament authors, he wrote, guided the people in their day by the right explanation and understanding of God's Word, they also occasionally proclaimed something concerning kings and worldly princes, and when doing so "they often erred." This erring never occurred in Scripture where anything to do with God's saving work was involved. So highly did Luther regard the authority of the Scripture that the call "Scripture alone" became a banner of the whole movement.

As he challenged the canon of biblical books inherited from the early church, he left no room for the Apocrypha, a collection of books that were influential in the church of Rome. He held controversial ideas about who wrote Ecclesiastes, Jude, Proverbs, and even parts of Genesis. In finding the books of Kings a hundred times better than the Chronicles, he was paying no compliment to the value of the books of Chronicles. As for the book of Revelation, the last in the New Testament, he wrote that his spirit could not make its way into it. One could not base a doctrine on any textual theme that appeared only in that apocalyptic document. Did the book of Esther belong in the canon? It did not even mention God. Though he liked the book of Hebrews, he was not sure it was canonical. Though the brother of Jesus wrote the Letter of James, Luther found it "right strawy," a book which contradicted the central Pauline teaching that one is saved by grace without the works of the law.

What mattered in all cases was that Scripture was, in his words, "most certain, more easy to understand, most clear, its own interpreter, testing, judging and illuminating everything by everything." In metaphors that he cherished, the Bible was the manger in which Christ lay, the swaddling clothes he wore. Luther called Christ the "central point of the circle around which everything else in the Bible revolves." Untroubled whenever he found an apparent discrepancy he could not resolve, he would urge readers to let it pass, since it did not endanger the articles of the Christian faith. Luther's summary was radical: "Therefore, if the adversaries press the Scriptures against Christ, we urge Christ against the Scriptures."

Both the Old Testament, written before Christ, and the New were authoritative because, as he put it, they pressed Christ. Rabbis, of course, always had to reject this view of the Old Testament as the book of Christ. It was their rejection that led Luther to engage in otherwise less explicable and never defensible denunciations of Jews and Judaism. On another front, those critics who appealed to church authority when they faced ambiguity or disagreed with him on items of biblical interpretation thought his treatment of the canon was subjective. He admittedly did call on the Holy Spirit and human experience to judge what was central when he made his choices within the canon. He preferred the Gospel of John to the other three gospels, because he found the preaching of Jesus there more important for faith than the stories elsewhere of the actions by Jesus. In that gospel the believer came to "have" Christ, while the other gospels were more "about" him, so he called John the one, fine, true, and chief gospel. The writings of Paul represented the other pole of the ellipse of teaching at the heart of the Bible for Luther.

When a moment came for summing up the changes in the church, he credited all to the Word. While he acknowledged that some of his friends, notably some princely supporters, deserved credit for translating, he offered a theological and gustatory interpretation: "I simply taught, preached and wrote God's Word; otherwise I did nothing. And while I slept, or drank Wittenberg beer with my friends Philip and Amsdorf, the Word so greatly weakened the papacy that no prince or emperor ever inflicted such losses upon it. I did nothing; the Word did everything."

The Word had more work to do, and Luther was poised for it. Now in his middle years, Professor Luther had to take on numerous unprofessorial roles, which in their variety issued in actions that kept chroniclers busy. In some of these we see him again as he saw the biblical Jacob, grappling with God and others and himself, necessarily inventing new holds when old grips failed him. He lacked training or expertise for many of these activities and, using his university education, his experience, and his wits, he could only improvise, yet he was defining all the while.

Especially when he expressed himself prematurely and brashly on the larger European scene he could overreach. Thus in one exceptional move he waged violent pamphlet warfare with England's King Henry VIII. In the complex interplay of political and military forces, the monarch had been trying to stay on good terms with the papacy, though he was soon to break away over his divorce and marital affairs. For the moment, the pope also had reason to deal gently with the king, who deduced that he was more likely to gain power in Europe if he kept papal favor. In 1521, no doubt with the help of clerics around him, Henry wrote a drab and meandering *Assertion of the Seven Sacraments.* This tract defending the seven sacraments attacked the Wittenbergers' views of the Lord's Supper. The pope thereupon officially named Henry Defender of the Faith.

Instead of letting the very ordinary treatise pass into well-deserved neglect, in June 1522 Luther published a screed, *Against Henry, King of England.* He justified his onslaught against this particular "effeminate" monarch on the grounds that Henry had attacked not Luther but Christ and the gospel. Fair-minded readers and cautious allies alike expressed regret over Luther's coarse and boasting language. Why, they asked, did he waste efforts making enemies through such an attack without exploiting any possibly compensatory chance to pick up friends or gain points? Evidently, for all his local gains, he felt alone, unsure, frustrated, and angered that the rulers who should by now have shared his version of the case against the papacy were not rallying to his message and appeal.

Charles meanwhile wanted desperately to enforce the Edict of Worms, but he was busy in Italy with wars against the always troubling nationalist Francis I of France. He dared not stir the evangelical princes of Germany into action that might disrupt his strategies. Luther had become a celebrity with whom rulers had to reckon. It is of interest to see how critics perceived him. Thus the Polish ambassador to the court of Charles V, Johannes Dantiscus, a cosmopolite who was later named bishop of Ermland, on his own initiative came to visit in the spring of 1523. While making his way home through Saxony after three years of service in Spain, he talked Melanchthon into arranging a meeting with the busy Luther after an evening meal.

Dantiscus opened their conversation with diplomatic words. It was coming to be believed, he said, that even if a person had seen the pope at Rome but never Luther, he had seen nothing at all. After a four-hour conversation advanced over wine and beer, he assessed his host as a man gifted with intelligence, learning, and eloquence, but one who arrogantly issued diatribes and cutting remarks when he discussed the pope, the emperor, and some princes. Luther looked to him like the portraits Dantiscus had seen. The eyes, he remarked, were piercing and sparkling. They displayed an eeriness that one might find in a person possessed. Since those eyes matched those of the king of Denmark, Luther and that king certainly had to have been born under the same astrological sign! Luther could be intense, sarcastic, and insinuating, but he also made excellent company drinking that beer and wine, as any good fellow thereabouts would do. All in all, Luther seemed almost respectable, but still he displayed to his guest an uneasiness that portended trouble.

Another example of Luther's growing awareness of a larger world came also in 1523, when he had to weep upon hearing that inquisitors burned at the stake two young Augustinians in Brussels. They had been testing the boundaries of the church and proclaiming the gospel of promise in the evangelical mode. Luther expressed regret that he had not been chosen to be the first martyr for the gospel on the new scene. Mourning the two "young boys," he next turned to verse and wrote his first published song, a brief narrative with epic intentions, one that anticipated his role as writer of hymns for worship and for home use. Faithful to the details of the burning, its text memorably portrayed the deaths not as a setback but as a victory for the gospel.

If we think of Luther as a specialist in dealing with matters of faith, we will find that he was a generalist when it came to leading in practical matters of church and state. Not a born administrator or theorist of governance, he improvised and often changed course. Personally, he began to signal that he did not identify himself as a priest. Thus in October 1524 he changed from wearing monastic garb to donning academic and street wear, symbolizing that he would abolish more distinctions among pastors and people. He also had to concern himself with funding the ministry of priests as they became pastors and worry about the supply of new pastors as the number of supporting congregations grew.

His evangelical churches had to revise the understanding of ranks in the church. Since he had declared that all baptized persons were at once, in effect, priests, bishops, and popes in the priesthood of all believers, some members wanted to set up shop as preaching heads of churches. What if congregations simply promoted any person of their own choice to lead them in preaching and also in sacramental observances? Luther, not wanting this to happen, was informal about church order but would not settle for chaos. The evangelicals had to establish some form of church order, but he insisted that they dared not claim that any of their choices was a unique divine creation prescribed in the Bible.

Looking left, Luther saw Thomas Müntzer and the Zwickau prophets creating disorder, while on the right the papacy governed through overly ordered policies. He complained: "Formerly the devil made us too papistic, and now he wants to make us too evangelical." He tried to make balanced decisions, as when in 1525, with no bishops ready to do so, he ordained student associate Georg Rörer for ministry in Wittenberg. He called it an emergency measure, but it became a precedent. For some time, along with Melanchthon, Luther seemed to think that the old connections with the bishops might be restored, and both welcomed the possibility that the episcopacy could remain to serve evangelical ends.

The issues had become how to connect evangelical parishes with one another and how to exercise oversight among them. Luther confessed: "We should have liked to erect again the genuine office of bishop and visitor, which is greatly needed." But being ordained by a bishop automatically made one a kind of junior officer in the Holy Roman Empire, and Luther and his followers abhorred that idea. Second, because bishops were members of a rank within a papal system that they rejected, the bishops were by definition too corrupt to satisfy evangelical intentions. Finally and practically, the old bishops simply would not ordain the ready candidates for the evangelical pulpits.

For an emergency substitute, Luther turned to princes in a letter whose groveling character has to be read because it contrasts so radically with the way he spoke to bishops: "We humbly and earnestly beg the serene, high-born, Prince John, Duke of Saxony, etc., our most gracious lord, ordained of God to be our country's prince and our earthly ruler . . . for the sake of God, the good of the gospel, and the benefit and salvation of the poor Christians in his dominions" graciously to "summon and appoint certain qualified persons to this office" of preaching and the pastorate. The high-born princes soon came to wield extraordinary power in the evangelical churches and showed themselves generally to be an inadequate replacement for the bishops in supervisory roles.

With princes in power in the church, Luther and his colleagues were forced to theorize more than before about the relations of church and state. The emperor, territorial princes, petty nobles, town magistrates, and others were civil governors amidst a diverse set of polities. Luther lumped them all together and spoke of them simply as temporal authority, seeing the state less as a legal institution than as an authority established by God for punishing evildoers and for serving citizens under the law of love for human good.

In a letter to Philip Melanchthon in 1521 Luther explained his developing thought. Regrettably, secular or temporal authorities had to keep order because true Christians were so few. Luther, with his realistic view of human nature, said he lacked trust in the goodness of Christian citizens. He could bend and stretch circumstances to become guilty of civil disobedience himself. When he chose to defy authorities, he explained that he was only defending the gospel. He had disobeyed his own prince, Frederick the Wise, when that elector did not want him to leave Wartburg and resume activities in Wittenberg. Luther explained that the Wittenberg work was for the gospel, so in that case he could resist authority and not face damnation. One could argue that his defiance of the emperor at Worms was also on the borderline between a defense of the gospel and civil disobedience.

In 1523, he aimed to provide guidance for rulers in *Temporal Authority: To What Extent Should It Be Obeyed?* The influence of Augustine was clear in such writing. Eleven hundred years earlier in *The City of God* Augustine intended to interpret emerging Christendom in relation to the Roman Empire. Luther found useful his distinguishing of the divine city, now represented in the church, from the temporal or earthly city. For governance, Luther mainly cited New Testament texts such as a passage in I Peter that commended, even commanded, obedience to proper earthly authority. In Romans 13 Paul demanded that Christians be subject to governmental powers. Only when the powers and authorities went against the gospel might they be disobeyed. Those who ruled on earth did so with the backing of God, and they possessed the sword to rule with the power of life and death. Those who resisted such authorities, wrote Paul and now Luther, would receive damnation.

Radically, Luther helped break the exclusive holds of church on state and state on church in the Roman system and the Holy Roman Empire. He drew a distinction between civil and spiritual authorities as part of his extremely influential theory of two *kingdoms*, which he distinguished from his accompanying theory of two *governments*. All believers live in two kingdoms. God created both, and both are under divine rule. Believers also live under two governments. God governs the church through the promise of the gospel, making people righteous. God governs human society through the divine law, expecting what Luther called civil righteousness. The human city therefore is not profane, not simply secular, never beyond the scope of God's activity.

Both nature and reason, Luther argued, should help guide the believer to respond positively to earthly authority. While all Christians always lived in the spheres of both kingdoms and under both governments, they had to learn to respond to God in different ways under the two rules. Luther wrote that Psalm 82 spelled out the limits of government, teaching believers that to rebuke rulers is not seditious, provided the rebuke comes in the way that the text described, through the "office" to which God committed that duty. Citizens were to speak publicly, boldly, and honestly to authority, and to rebuke rulers in this way, he concluded, was "a praiseworthy, noble, and rare virtue, and a particularly great service to God."

Circling around princes who served the papal Antichrist, Luther wrote for Christian princes. They must always use reason and realize how high were the stakes in their decisions. He claimed that he did not have sufficient knowledge about law and governing to counsel rulers on exactly how to put reason to work for justice. He wrote that he only wanted to instruct the heart of the prince. Therefore, predictably, he advised temporal authorities to be prayerfully confident in God and then to treat their subjects with love and serve them as Christians. The apostle Paul, he added, had prescribed that such rulers should punish evildoers for the sake of order but, speaking to their hearts, Luther advised them to punish too little rather than too much.

Finally, since princes so regularly made war against each other, Luther had to address military dilemmas. While some of the evangelical radicals were pacifist, Luther did allow that Christians might have to participate in war. He counseled that they should work for peace and devoted a few lines at least to an issue that would trouble many people of conscience. In them he told soldiers that, if wars were necessary and unavoidable, they had to follow commands into bloody defensive conflicts. Yet when a ruler sent them into battles that they knew to be unjust, they must refuse to fight and then face the consequences. Killing in such wars was murder.

Luther was smug about the way he had defined the interrelations of the two kingdoms to each other as well as the two governments, also to each other. Three years after writing on this subject he boasted that "not since the time of the apostles have the temporal sword and temporal government been so clearly described or so highly praised as by me. Even my enemies must admit that." He did not interview Duke George to gain his assent to that claim.

All the while Luther was writing and urging people to fear the temporal sword and to obey government, fearless and disobedient antigovernment forces were gathering in actions that led him to the most controversial secular involvement of his life. In his strident pamphlets against them, these neighbors came to be known simply as the peasants and their revolt in 1524–25 became the Peasants' War. The figure of Luther had become so central to life in the territories where their revolt broke out that he could not evade appeals to take sides.

Not all those who lived in peasant circumstances were desperately poor, but many of them sided with the urban poor and were rightfully resentful of unjust taxes, including church revenues. In the eyes of those poor, anyone like Luther who criticized the established church's policies should have been their friend. He talked of Christian freedom and they wanted to claim their version of it. What is more, he sometimes liked to identify himself as being of peasant ancestry, thus giving the impression that he might be able to empathize with peasants who, by any standard, had justifiable grievances. As the princes expropriated lands that the church once owned, many of them plundered and used the yield selfishly instead of sharing it with the peasants who had worked the soil and must live off it. While by this time the days of feudal society were numbered, there was still plenty of life among those who had the power to keep some of it in place. They were used to having their way when setting prices or prohibiting poachers on their preserves— the penalty for poaching being death—and they had the superior forces of arms.

Luther turned his back on the peasants. What erupted in military action by ill-equipped rebels in the summer of 1524 and came to a climax between March and May of the next year was an early and local outburst of rage. In March 1525 some peasants in the region publicly presented their protest in the form of Twelve Articles, which included an appeal to Scripture and to the new Christian movements that preached grace and freedom on the basis of their understanding of the Bible. Luther responded negatively to even the moderate demands. Believers as Christians, in his argument, should adjust and make do with the cards dealt them in the rigged but desperately serious games of societal life.

Some authorities read Luther's confusing acts and writings as signs that he himself was now already losing influence and control. They saw him trying futilely to restrain the very revolutionary forces that he had helped unleash. If the peasants would succeed in their revolts and disorder would follow, he wrote in virtual panic, both the spiritual and temporal spheres of life would be destroyed and there would be neither worldly government nor Word of God. Authority and order must win, while chaos would thwart the preaching of the gospel of the kingdom of God. To Luther the revolt was one more sign that the world was in its last days.

Luther, advising that God did not favor rule by ordinary people, discerned to his own satisfaction that it was the devil who so quickly seized so many thousands of peasants, deceived them, blinded them, hardened them, threw them into revolt, and did with them whatever his raging fury undertook. Luther heard many stories of peasant ferocity and atrocity. The princes, already good at killing, did not need encouragement as they attacked Thuringian rebels, thousands of whom fell. Luther, a theological rebel himself, told the princes and others who opposed the peasants that they should let everyone who can, smite, slay, and stab, secretly or openly, remembering that nothing could be more poisonous, hurtful, or devilish than a rebel. His comparisons were gross: "It is just as when one must kill a mad dog; if you do not strike him, he will strike you, and a whole land with you."

Luther after some time did note the degree to which the princes were also agents of tumult. He severely scolded them, but his calls for restraint, most of them coming too late, were not very effective. The peasants were disorganized, poorly armed, badly led, easily confronted, and vulnerable to frightful defeats. They grabbed for ideology or help wherever they could find it—even from witches, some said, if no one else was around. They needed a strong and somehow credible leader and thought they found him in Thomas Müntzer. That stormy utopian preacher spoke for prophets who identified their cause with God's and spread unrealizable expectations among the discontented, offering them powers that were beyond their reach and thus exposing them to fatal dangers. The fact that the rebels were siding with radicals like Müntzer only led Luther to despise the peasants further. He knew that if he wanted to be regarded as any kind of friend to princes, he had reason to take this stand, since it was well known that Müntzer asked peasants to kill rulers and never let their blood dry on the rebels' weapons.

Luther shared many of the prejudices that the educated and better-off people around him directed against peasants as a class. To him, they often looked stupid, illiterate, money hungry, dirty, and slow to respond to the gospel. When they did become alive to God's promise, he thought that most got everything wrong. They looked for temporal victories, while he wanted to stress the promise of deferred benefits in the life to come. How, he asked, could peasant leaders credibly have used his *The Freedom of a Christian* as a license for the kind of freedom they now craved? Why did they think he had written *The Babylonian Captivity of the Church* but to free hungry souls from what it was that troubled them? His words in these tracts now sounded like wake-up calls that should have better left them sleeping. After the denouement Luther tried to help pick up some of the pieces, but never again could he win the favor of peasants as a group. They had been losing ground before the war. Now, suffering even more after it, they became leaderless and were unable to mount a cause.

Years later, according to a recorder of his conversations, which were published under the title *Table Talk*, Luther cavalierly and cruelly took much of the blame or credit for a complex set of incidents in the Peasants' War that included the rape of women, who were left to die; the stringing up of men on trees; the death of children in the cold of winter; and perhaps the taking of 100,000 lives in all: "Preachers are the greatest of slayers. For they urge the authorities to execute their office strictly and punish the wicked. In the revolt I slew all the peasants; all their blood is on my head. But I pass it on to our Lord, who commanded me to speak thus."

Authorities who had been resisting change now found satisfying evidence that change was dangerous. After months of turmoil it was clear that the peasants had lost everything while most princes, only some of them slightly chastened by Luther, still ruled arbitrarily. Meanwhile, on May 2, 1525, his protector Frederick the Wise died, so the preacher and professor who also had become a political figure had to begin to cultivate relations with Frederick's brother John the Steadfast, the new elector. Whether he had wanted to or not, Luther had become a public figure pushed onto the stage of European statecraft, untutored and unready, but willing where he thought the defense and spread of the gospel were at stake.

CHAPTER THREE

Living the Faith

1525–1530

IN 1525, THE FORTY-TWO-YEAR-OLD LUTHER, now a renowned public figure, turned attention to his private life and to that of his immediate community. Most surprisingly, soon after he published a notorious tract, *Against the Murderous and Thieving Peasants*, he announced his betrothal to an escaped nun, Katherine von Bora, whom he wed in June. His attacks on priestly celibacy, his views of Christian vocation, and his praise of marriage frame the story of these two events.

To violate the rule of priestly celibacy meant to repudiate centuries not of theology but of practical precedent. Already in the early Christian church some leaders combined negative views of sexual expression with positive views of what a spouseless cleric could achieve for God. In 1123 the Lateran Council mandated clerical celibacy as an aid to church reform. The restrictive policy was designed in part to deal with a property problem. Christian people often deeded estates to the church or paid clergy to say Mass for the dead. Clerics who pocketed significant sums and even benefited from corrupt landholding policies acquired wealth that they would pass on to heirs.

The law of celibacy, for all the flaws connected with it, was so deeply etched on the minds of the faithful and so strongly did church leaders insist on it that to question it and then to promote clerical marriage struck very close to the social foundations of the church and government. Of course, Christians could—or at least they had to—tolerate all kinds of corruptions of the practice. Many hierarchical leaders of the church immediately before the time of Luther lived in open liaisons with mistresses and fathered illegitimate children. To violate the rule of celibacy as many clergy did was one thing. To set out to abolish it was another, a rare and extreme consideration.

Luther did not attack celibacy wholesale. He said he would have little complaint if only unwed monks led holy lives, though he grumbled that many took vows in order to get right with God and to be saved through their works. Like his contemporary Erasmus, he denounced the lawless clergy who went whoring or kept concubines. Unlike Erasmus, he then went on to affirm sexual life, while advocating that the religiously dedicated should marry. Before long he was waving good-bye to colleagues on their way from the cloister to the altar and was welcoming them with their spouses soon after, as they began wedded life.

In a letter written in November 1524 to court chaplain Georg Spalatin, Luther pointed out that he was also free to marry and might indeed wed. Being neither wood nor stone, as he put it, he had not stayed single because he was unaware of his flesh or his masculine sexuality. He told Spalatin he hoped that God would not have him live alone. Luther may have been slow to marry simply because he was busy, politically preoccupied, and spiritually engrossed, but he mentioned one other reason. Excommunicated and hunted, he daily faced the prospect of capture. Though a benign elector temporarily protected him, he was still in effect under a death sentence. Since he could and very well might lose that protection and thus his life, he had to ask whether he dared jeopardize the future of a potential life partner.

Still another reason for holding back had to do with his view of history. God's time for humans to repent had run out. The advance of the Turk toward central Europe, the activities of the papal Antichrist, and numbers of other signs suggested to him that time for the Last Day was near. He brought up this apocalyptic thought not to discourage others from making the best use of their own last days by marrying but because he thought marriage would distract him personally from fulfilling his mission. Gradually he overcame his reluctance to take the step toward marriage. Thus on May 4, in the same letter in which he urged a member of the town council to resist the warring peasants, he calmly announced that to spite the devil he might marry Katherine von Bora.

His critics taunted: Was this ex-monk undercutting the practice of the whole church and breaking his monastic vows just because his sinful flesh had gotten the better of him? Or if marriage had not occurred to him in his first forty-one years, how could he wed so blithely in his forty-second? Critics were sure he was moved only by uncontrollable sexual drives. He did admit that he experienced some nocturnal emissions "of physical necessity," and as a normal man he admitted to some sexual yearnings, but he said he did not even look at girls when they came to confession.

In the advice he gave and the turn he took Luther was contributing to a new concept of vocation, or "calling," which in a different version had been a central theme in his clerical culture. Few of his teachings or discoveries carried more consequence than this for indicating what the life of faith meant. To begin with, to replace the monastic version of vocation he came up with an alternative concept which, while including much more than marriage, certainly made room for it. For several years he rejected approaches that restricted the idea of a calling to those who took monastic or priestly vows. If in a monastic vocation a particular person could serve his or her neighbor, well and good. But to make the decision to profess a vow in order to seek divine favor and to merit grace had to be of the devil.

Luther inherited an old ethic of holiness in which God looked with special favor on those who prayed constantly and abased themselves. His new teaching challenged this ethic. He made his point by using imagery that shocked: The mother suckling the baby and washing diapers, the farmer at work, the couple having sex were as likely to be engaged in God-pleasing activities as was any nun engaged in prayer. Luther secondly made a distinction between the honored way that one lives out a calling in the professions, jobs, tasks, and roles here below on earth and the also honored way that the same person receives a calling from God through the grace which relates to life above in heaven. Only gospel, never God's law, had a part to play in the second of these. The laws for life here below applied inescapably to all, be they princes or peasants, people at prayer or cleansing the stables, working hard or finding amusement, procreating or grieving, peacefully serving justice or fighting in just wars.

The key for judging life here below had less to do with whether the agent was a believer destined for life above and eternally with God than with whether he or she temporally served the purposes of God through being of help to others. Those who were of such use, in Luther's eyes, were themselves masks of God, since God was hidden within every person's vocation. Therefore, believers and unbelievers alike could be cooperators with God in matters of civil righteousness, but none of them could cooperate with God to achieve personal Christian righteousness.

To take the immediate illustration of all this as being relevant to the Luthers: When married couples enjoyed making love to each other, they could also be fulfilling a vocation and serving God. Sometimes Luther's writings on such points sound more like an attack on existing church laws and practices than like a defense of marriage, but defend it he did. Seven years had gone by since he rejected his own monastic commitment, and two years had elapsed since he helped engineer the escape of eleven nuns from the nearby Nimmschen convent. As he busied himself talking others into marrying the refugees from the monastery, it must have occurred to Luther the matchmaker to appraise one or another and woo her as a potential spouse. Finally he chose Katherine von Bora, from a family that had ties to nobility but were now anything but well off. A strong-willed woman, Katherine rejected some suitors and had been rejected by one other and was thus coming to the point where marriage seemed unlikely. Only two of the available men were attractive to her, and the one she favored was Martin Luther.

With that frame for a setting, here is the picture of the betrothal on June 13, the ceremony at which couples were considered to be marrying in the sight of God: John Bugenhagen officiated, with five witnesses present, among them artist Lucas Cranach and his wife, Barbara. Friend Justus Jonas next drew duty upstairs to observe the copulation, a formal term for the sealing of the betrothal bond. In most cases this accompanied the formal wedding instead of the betrothal ceremony. Couples in the Saxon culture of the day were to be witnessed thrashing around on the marital bed demonstrating that they had achieved consummation. Breakfast followed. On June 27 the Luthers processed to the church for the marriage blessing and followed it with a marriage feast at which the groom's delighted parents were present.

Luther, never shy, was almost tasteless when he brought talk of marital intimacies into the open. He seems to have been a robust lover more than a romantic one. Sometimes he treated sex instrumentally and even connected conjugal activity with efforts to overcome one of the seven deadly sins. That sin was sloth, which referred not to laziness but to the experience of listlessness of the soul, sadness in the face of spiritual good. Luther remarked later that when such sloth assailed him, he faced depression by lying next to and holding God's instrument—his wife Katherine's nude body. Still, he knew that however delightful he found Katherine to be as she slept next to him, he could still be assailed by *Anfechtungen*. These he attributed not to the sexual sphere as such but to demonic challenges to his faith.

Luther was distancing himself from the Augustinian vision that saw sexual congress to be necessary for childbearing but intrinsically lustful. He viewed it as a positive expression and even introduced elements of play into talk about lovemaking. In a letter of December 1525, he encouraged his friend Spalatin to wed and thereupon urged the couple to make love. Spalatin should find divine grace, peace in the Lord, and joy with his sweet little wife. Luther counseled that when the couple embraced and kissed, Spalatin was to think of her as the best creation God had given him in Christ. Luther capped the letter with a bit of erotic calculation as he determined a night and a time when the Spalatins and the Luthers, though miles apart, could make love at the same hour. Each should meanwhile also think of the other couple in embrace. That counsel, if followed, would have left the lovers partially distracted, but it does reveal something affirmative about Luther's regard for the body and marital love.

If through the years there was ever a major conflict between the Luthers, it did not enter the records. Martin could speak in ironic terms of Katherine as the one who ruled over him, because she so well governed the household. His letters often included joshing and terms of endearment. Taking off from comments on biblical patriarchs and their fondling of spouses—Isaac relating to Rebekah was a case in point—Luther wrote that "with the woman who has been joined to me by God I may jest, have fun, and converse more pleasantly."

As much as he honored wives, he still did little to counter the inherited understanding that the woman was subordinate to the man and even continued to hold that opinion himself. With so many in his time, he considered that because the husband had a strong sexual drive, he needed to satisfy it by entering his wife, but Luther advocated the rights of both and encouraged both to find pleasure. In two theoretical but drastic situations he counseled first that if a woman persistently denied her man, the husband might then turn to the housemaid or someone else for sexual relations. He balanced that provocative and patriarchal advice with its counterpart: A woman who was wed to an impotent man but who desired to have children or was unable to remain continent, "with the consent of the man (who is not really her husband, but only a dweller under the same roof with her)," should have intercourse with another, for example her husband's brother. They were to keep this "marriage" secret and ascribe any children to the "so-called putative father." Such a woman would be in a saved state and would not be displeasing God.

One does not expect romantic effusions from someone like Luther, but it is obvious that he was affectionate in marriage and childrearing. Katherine, who was not especially attractive, struck many as being overly assertive. Her husband foresaw that no doubt she would stand up to him, as she often did in the Black Cloister, which became their home. They had to work together to survive without the basic economic support that monks and nuns in community could expect. Early on some friends offered gifts to the virtually penniless couple. Cardinal Archbishop Albrecht of Brandenburg (a relative of Luther's nemesis Cardinal Albrecht of Mainz) nobly sent twenty gulden and two silver goblets. Martin considered these to be unneeded luxuries, so Katherine took it in hand to hide the goblets, thus to keep him from being able to sell them.

While little is known about Katherine's life apart from the illuminating records of Luther and the students who crowded the table, a consistent portrait appears. She took over and tidied up the house. The husband told of his shock in the early days of marriage and his enjoyment later when he woke to find pigtails on the pillow next to his. That pillow was clean; he reported that they slept in a good bed. Monastery-housed Luther confessed that he had long tumbled into bed so weary that for many months he did not air his moldy, perspiration-clotted straw mattress. Neglect of personal hygiene had to end when efficient Katherine took command.

Just as with marriage, so Luther saw childbearing and -rearing as mandates in a vocation. Having valued sexual expression as part of marital love, he honored it more because it helped couples fulfill the divine command to have children and to realize God's blessings that came with them. He therefore saw Kate's presence to be in continuity with that of the first mother, noting that without Eve and her breasts no other institution would have come to be. Hoping to procreate also for the sake of the yearnings for grandchildren on the part of his long-suffering parents, he worried in the early months of marriage that the couple might not have children. It turned out that they were well enough matched in bed, and children came soon. A first son was born in June 1526, a little more than a year after the wedding day. A second one who followed in another year did not survive. By 1534 there had been six children, four of whom survived.

Seldom did the Luther family have the Black Cloister all to themselves. They took income from boarding students and hosted regular nonpaying guests at the table. Some diners took notes and assembled book-length collections of what they called Luther's *Table Talk*, which was sometimes pithy and often provocative comment on informal and personal matters. Luther tried to provide income through gardening, which he enjoyed, and woodworking, but he failed in both efforts, so he counted on Katherine to be a working mother who brought in income and kept the household accounts. She did all this with reasonable readiness and considerable skill. For that income and to procure household necessities, she bred pigs, brewed beer, and grew vegetables. One sign of her acumen in bookkeeping and stewardship came near the end of the Luther story. Departing from the custom of the day, Martin in his will appointed only Katherine to oversee their modest estate, trusting her to provide for herself and the children. This she did.

While records of warm parent-child relations from their

culture are sparse, and discipline more than affection was to mark the ties, Luther demonstrated real love for the couple's children. When in her early adolescence his favorite, Magdalena, died, he was inconsolable and almost lost the ability to sustain the life of faith. He even spoke of losing his faith for a time, something he never did when he faced and had to fear the hatred and power of popes, emperors, and princes. On the more positive side, his literary legacy also included a delightful letter he wrote son Hans. In it he described the pleasures of heaven in terms of a garden full of playthings that would delight a child's imagination. The verdict on the married couple and the family was that overall they were happy and rewarded. The word Luther liked to use for his attitude toward Katherine was that he esteemed her, and he had good reason to.

However healing to Luther's soul was the nearness of bedmate Katherine's unclad body and however consoling the presence of children, in the early years of his marriage he also began to experience intensified physical illness. Whenever he took inventory of his body or when pain assaulted him, he would speak of his desire to die. Uncertain in the face of the threats of earthly life, especially during an outbreak of the plague, he professed certainty only in faith. Once in a letter to his father he explained why he did not finally fear death: Our faith is certain, he wrote, and believers, in this case father and son, did not doubt that they would meet soon again after death in Christ.

With Katherine cooking and Martin eating, he also became overweight. He never took good care of himself during his times of presence at or absence from her table. He reported in 1525 that a wound on his leg that had not healed for years often troubled him. In sickness and in health he did keep preaching, but congregations found him pausing in sermons when headaches, dizziness, or fainting spells afflicted him. During and after such attacks his ears would ring and he would be subject to chills and fever. After one terrifying seizure, he said, he was on the verge of falling into despair and blasphemy and feared that he had lost Christ. The physician and the prayerful congregants under his pulpit were then in his eyes God's agents of mercy who rescued him from hell. So in illness or health, he plunged ahead through the private dark passages of midlife.

Beyond the home, the next circle was the local church, an immediate sphere in which to develop the life of faith. Any visitors who in the late 1520s might walk into a church that followed the patterns and orders encouraged by Luther and his colleagues and could compare these to the sights and sounds of worship in the same building a dozen years earlier would have found dramatic contrasts. Most notably, the pulpit now occupied a central or lofty place for the preaching of the Word. Communicants received bread *and* wine. The people sang hymns in vernacular languages that replaced Latin. Before they left the house of God on a Sunday, young and old alike in a catechism class might also have learned some doctrines and counsel about behavior.

Beyond his focus on the centrality of the promise of God, Luther regarded much else as negotiable. He thought of himself as being quite conservative in the ways of worship, and in most respects he was. Let Müntzer and the radicals down the road upset everything; he would not. No, he urged, don't let them upset *anything*. He and his Wittenberg colleagues opposed the actions of some extremists who, like the radicals in the city of Münster in Westphalia, in search of what they thought of as pagan idols left over from the pope's rule, trampled images, broke stained-glass windows, and destroyed pipe organs. Luther scorned the iconoclasts and to some degree valued the visual arts, counting artists as notable as the Elder and Younger Cranachs in his most intimate circle.

He addressed preaching again and further defined it, thinking of it as a kind of sacrament of sound waves. For him the sermon was not a lecture that described God but an announcement of a gift that offered God and God's benefits to human ears and hearts. Preached messages that were well grounded in Scripture texts were seen themselves as events of grace. This concept put great pressure on preachers, not all of whom were up to their task. When they were made aware of their own limits as speakers, preachers were to stir congregants by reading one of the Postils, printed sermons by Luther. Frail as the instrument of the sermon seemed to be against the power of pope and emperor, it rallied the people sufficiently to lead them into understandings of a very different kind of church in a new Europe.

Worship was not merely a preaching matter. Congregations were to respond in prayer, praise, and music in the form of songs and hymns. Music gave Luther a chance to demonstrate another element of living the Christian life, whether at home or in formal worship. For centuries the chief music of worship had been in the hands and came from the voices of chanting monks and clerics. Now in evangelical churches of all sorts, while instrumental music and choirs were familiar fixtures, most of the singing came from lay worshipers. A lutenist who liked to accompany song, Luther in 1524 wrote the first of his surviving hymns, "Dear Christians, One and All Rejoice," and numerous others followed. Pleading for writers to come forth with simple music, he contended that since the people were supposed to be united in worship they would best respond in song to the preached Word.

Luther elaborated: "I have no use for cranks who despise music, because it is a gift of God. Music drives away the Devil and makes people gay; they forget thereby all wrath, unchastity, arrogance, and the like. Next after theology I give to music the highest place and the greatest honor." In fact, he elaborated, "experience proves that next to the Word of God only music deserves to be extolled as the mistress and governess of the feelings of the human heart." Because he trusted music to help build community, he would sputter and fume when congregations would neither readily learn hymns nor even care to become familiar with them. He once charged that after the message of the gospel first reached their congregations, apathetic Wittenbergers could have enjoyed two or three years of fresh opportunity to sing but, he complained, they still acted like tone-deaf sluggards.

On one occasion in his home as Luther listened to

motets he responded with a flourish: "If our Lord God has given us such noble gifts in the outhouse of this life, what will there be in that life eternal where everything will be perfect and delightful?" For the in-house of worship life, he wrote rhymed versions of some parts of the liturgy and also provided more chorales of his own. The new hymns, picking up as they did on folk and popular music, were not repetitious phrases but often narratives that reinforced the gospel stories or that were reworkings of Psalms. Together they became the martial music of advancing evangelical believers in company with one another. Despite the apathy of many congregants, he and his colleagues kept investing in the music through which the evangelical movement proceeded. Not far from Wittenberg in Torgau, Johann Walther, the first evangelical church cantor, supplied some chorales or hymns that became classics, and Walther soon had company among providers of the noble gifts of music.

While the gospel was supposed to rule in the regard marital partners had for each other, and while it was the subject of preaching and hymnody, in a third dimension of Christian living Luther and his colleagues, in partial contradiction to their main profession and intention, often fell back on the law. The best way to observe this dimension is in the development of church governance, the education of Christian children, and, most important, the visitations of congregations.

As for governance, Luther judged that if a pattern of polity or policy did not stand in the way of the gospel there could be flexibility in church order. For some local congregations, Luther and his colleagues provided at least rudimentary ordinances, beginning with experiments at the town of Leisnig in 1523. These prescriptions dealt with congregational teaching, doctrine, efforts to influence morality, and acts of tending to the poor, encouraging family life, and promoting public education.

Fortunately, while no bishops turned to the evangelical cause, numerous Saxon and Thuringian princes and their counterparts in other territories did support it and were available for their strange new role of taking on many tasks bishops once held. Pressure grew on the evangelicals to bring coherence to church order. Prussia, north of Saxony, was the first territory to produce a pattern of evangelical church administration under Albrecht of Brandenburg. As churches in Prussia fell into line, so did those in Hesse and Saxony.

In 1525 leaders of church and state inaugurated a pattern of visitations among congregations. Princes appointed visitors to check on the condition of the churches within their lands, inspections that they deemed crucial for the health of the evangelical movement. Visitors called on local church leaders to give an account of themselves and their flocks. They were expected to be alert to abuses, such as when landed nobles seized monasteries and other church property for themselves instead of turning it over to the economically stretched evangelical congregations. Luther was especially concerned about the low wages on which the new pastors had to live. For him and the visitors, however, priests who had become pastors also were expected to shape up. They heard pointed and urgent questions: Did these clerics lead moral lives? Were they now ready to marry the women with whom they had sired children back when they were priests? Luther and the visitors sometimes embarrassed clergy into making public announcements that they were indeed marrying their former mistresses. The main inquiries of visitors, however, dealt with the question of whether pastors were preaching the promises of God, and Luther often had doubts about how well they were doing this.

Since the empowered princes were not to treat doctrine and most could not handle subtleties of theology or showed little interest in them, some pastors from larger centers took up the slack and came to be superintendents. Since the word *bishop* meant overseer or superintendent, it was turning out that the evangelical congregations were now developing an episcopal system of supervision. Apparent contradictions marked church order. In 1520 Luther declared that when faith, as in the case of baptismal faith, is present, "all Christian men are priests, all women priestesses, be they young or old, master or servant, mistress or maid, learned or unlearned." But he became uneasy after reading reports that some heads of households and other laypeople took it upon themselves to administer the Lord's Supper in homes or churches. In criticism he wrote: "It is true that all Christians are priests, but not all are pastors." He and his colleagues insisted that the church called ministers not to a rank but to an office in which they should administer the sacraments. They did not detail extensive biblical warrants for this position.

As a visitor or reader of visitation reports, Luther lost faith in the ability of locals to be their own superintendents, so he did not resist when the princes filled the vacuum. Thereupon another of the contradictions in Luther's polity and practice appeared. The church was supposed to be ruled by the gospel, yet in several leading capacities the highest officers of human law held express authority in the church and ruled by law. Whether law-based government by princes and town councils was congruent with Luther's own vision of life under the gospel was debatable from the first day. He wanted churches and their leaders to get on with the preaching of the gospel, the instruction of the young, the improvement of moral and disciplined life, and the challenge of living in expectation of Judgment Day. He was signaling, not always subtly, however, that if it took princes to help enforce by law what was supposed to have been part of a voluntary assent to the gospel, so be it.

Elements of corruption entered the system. Patronage came along with political leadership as middle-level town councillors and lower-level nobles often filled supervisory gaps between princes and congregations. There are signs that Luther did not favor the emergent pattern, but since he had not come up with an effective alternative, he tried to head off the worst by working with Philip Melanchthon, who wrote "Instructions for the Visitors," which Luther used as a standard for inspectors. To make things come out to their satisfaction, Luther and Melanchthon as leaders first reminded themselves that the princes were, after all, or first of all, baptized believers. Second, as princes they were also to be thought of as the prime members of the church. Who had better credentials than these to put the church in order?

Here was a lapse. Anyone who might picture potent princes being self-restrained in the exercise of spiritual power would have needed a sunnier view of human nature than the Wittenberg leaders possessed and proclaimed. Apparently contradicting one of Luther's motifs without evoking significant questions from him, Melanchthon charged princes to enforce the law of God when they discovered departures in congregational life. For the most part congregants themselves shared in governing only in theory, no matter how much Luther would have wanted to see them lead in practice. Agencies that were anything like effective parish councils were rare.

Luther was often dismayed by the visitation reports. As he did so often, he connected disconcerting evidences of shortcomings in practical church life with the belief that the world was coming to an end. Awareness of Judgment Day, he thought, should have produced new attitudes of mind among evangelical believers, inspiring communicants to re order their lives before they met God. The baptized Saxons, upon hearing the pure gospel, should have hurried to the communion table, eagerly listened to the Word, and enjoyed lives of evangelical piety in the service of others. Though they certainly had welcomed the liberating note in his earlier preaching and pamphleteering, now many were turning out to be indifferent, wayward, even wicked.

The visitation reports made clear, for instance, that many evidenced very weakly the life of faith. Pastors and members often changed very little from their practices under the Roman system. After a dozen years of evangelical preaching, Justus Jonas claimed to find that under their robes, in their hearts, many priests, now pastors, really cherished the old ways but were eager for the salaries, meager though these were, that might come with their new situations. Many new pastors were as drunk and immoral as were the priests they once had been or whom they replaced. And many laypeople were anything but capable of rendering their weak faith active in love or responding to calls for justice. Luther continued to want to rely on the promise of God, but he had to shelve some of his principles and resort to the law, as when the princes and their agents in the territories of the Holy Roman Empire, with his consent, rounded up children and forced them to attend catechism classes.

Though the Last Day was at hand and could soon come, Luther did give attention to the nurture of new generations in whatever remained of the world's future. To implement his goal, he made education of the young an urgent concern. That is why it was all right with him for the princes to coerce children into the sphere of gospel teaching. Luther displayed another set of contradictions when he advised how to treat the young as they learned to live the Christian life. He saw infants and very young children as relative innocents who could well be molded to lead good lives if adults would be gentle and attentive. Perhaps recalling the times when his parents had been harsh with him, he wrote that fathers should raise children in ways that would lead them never to lose trust. A loving God was to be the model for this approach. On the milder side, often making reference to his own role as a parent, Luther advocated that adults use play and games to lure their children into voluntary patterns of learning and obedience. Experiences with his own children sometimes led him to evoke rosy pictures of infancy. As he watched his offspring play, he declared that he thought they faced heaven without doubt in their hearts. They were good candidates for receiving the gospel.

At the same time—in respect to Luther one so often says "at the same time"—he held dark views of children and their nature. A line from Genesis 8:21 that he readily quoted stated that children, like everyone else, harbored evil inclinations. Then he watched the not really innocent children as they developed and illustrated the darker sides of their nature. By age five, he observed, they were given to laziness and frivolity instead of to willing obedience or discipline. By the time the children had grown up, the once apparently angelic young creatures could also act like old devils.

Education helped bring forth some of the better sides of the child's nature. Luther believed so much in training the young that he sometimes seemed to be giving up on adults. Since it was necessary to start all over with children if one wanted to revive the church, he also paid much attention to the education of young girls, though he lost much of his interest in their learning when they reached their teens and young adulthood. He stressed education in Christian faith but also promoted the liberal arts in general. His teaching on vocations, which included the call to participate in civic or public life, led him to stress the role of education in preparing children for their callings. To that end, he pioneered in advocating public education at a time when such support was rare.

As for the development of the young, he pictured that Christian nurture should begin with the most intimate setting, the family. Parents who failed to teach, failed their children. The next step up was the local congregation. Of course, the university also had its special role in respect to developing an informed citizenry. If the church could not do the educating, the state must take over. Those who governed would be given no excuse; they could not evade their educational task. If they were neglectful, Luther declared that Elector John of Saxony, whom he called the supreme guardian of the young people, would have to intervene.

Luther here seemed to be losing faith that the gospel by itself would inspire action, saying instead that where people did not care enough about their own salvation, the elector had ample power to compel them to hear the Word and teach children. If the prince was capable of summoning armies to fight, he certainly ought to be able to find what Luther called the greater force to compel parents to send their children to school. Children, in his view, were really only on loan to parents; God was their real owner. Governments should therefore punish parents who neglected to bring their children to Christian schooling. Having written the Leisnig people in 1523 that the common good of the public could make a higher demand on children than could their parents, he held to that claim.

For the rest, in the world of citizens and in the sphere of

justice, the neighbor's need and not the character or quality of belief was to determine policy and practice. As for the enjoyment of life, believers could live out their vocations with special freedom, since faith and grace had taken care of life above. God wanted humans to enjoy present things and, as he phrased it, with joyous and pleasant mind be without solicitude and care concerning things to come. He devoted himself zealously to the role of educating so that people could serve God in positions that could be best described by the word *secular*, which meant belonging to things below.

However much he focused on the secular realm, Luther was still most concerned with education in the ways of the gospel. To further this in 1529 he produced a classic *Small Catechism*. Behind this short work for laity stood the sturdier *Large Catechism*, a substantial book that condensed Luther's main themes. It was to be an instruction manual for pastors, preachers, and teachers. Without such a manual he feared that believers would be ill equipped to go about their work, especially since so many of them had grown up apart from the approaches advocated by the preachers of Wittenberg. Of course, the Bible was to determine everything, but the Bible was a long book with many stories that did not relate to the foundations of faith and nurture. The catechisms highlighted the basic elements.

Luther's catechisms, which offered patterned summaries of inherited and now refreshed church teaching, inspired many imitators. The shorter catechism, which appeared in question-and-answer form, was memorable and memorizable, better than the large one for the instruction of children on those basics of faith. Luther claimed that he himself read in his own catechism daily, and the claim might well have been true.

The first surprise to anyone encountering the instructional works is the amount of space—more than half of *The Large Catechism*—that he gave to the Ten Commandments. Since Luther so regularly said that no one could be saved by obeying the Commandments and that everything depended on the gospel, his strong accent on the law of God seems curious, and in the eyes of some even misplaced. He may have been looking over his shoulder at new and rival movements called Antinomian, which meant adherents thought that the law of God had no place in Christian life once one received the grace of the gospel.

Luther himself told why he made much of the Commandments. He spoke chiefly of two uses of the law of God. The political use had to do with maintaining order and pursuing justice on earth. The theological use served to accuse sinners and drive them to God's promise. While Melanchthon favored also a third use of the law, Luther discouraged it. This third use was to be pedagogical, as it would provide a guide or a rule for reborn believers. This Luther thought unnecessary, because if the love of God was present in believers and if they had knowledge of the first or civil use of the law, nothing more was necessary, while more might confuse them.

In the second use, then, when people tried to follow the Commandments in order to become right with God, the law always and only accused and terrified them. Making sinners feel helpless and hopeless apart from grace, divine law was creative, because having truly heard it they would be driven to rely on the promises of God through faith. The law of God, he taught, revealed the gap between human life at its best and the exacting divine demands. Yet Luther also described appropriate ways of life in his explanation of responses to the Commandments. Apart, then, from the issue of using the law in order to become righteous, it was still a message of God that promoted human good.

Commenting on the Apostles' Creed, as Luther did in both catechisms, gave him his best opportunity to bring to focus the central themes of faith. His explanations are remarkably personal. Of course, the God professed in the creed was Creator of the whole universe, but believers, he instructed, should learn first to note the wonders of their own bodies, their reason and senses, and then to ponder how God preserved them. Thereupon followed claims that everything from good government to good weather flowed from the divine act of creation. To read Luther's theology in the light of what he taught about the Apostles' Creed is to learn how intoxicated he was with the idea and practice of letting God be God. The five-word translation of his comment each time he explained the three articles of the creed also show how the searcher for certainty through faith conceived as trust also claimed it for faith in doctrine: "This is most certainly true."

Because they reflected personal concerns, some paragraphs in the catechisms served well for those who wanted to make sense of various aspects of Luther's life. The author of the catechism assumed that his own experiences could serve as a template by which other readers might interpret their own. As one illustration, *The Large Catechism* shows him helping others wrestle as he himself did with doubt and temptation. He cast the drama of ordinary life against a cosmic backdrop in which the devil as tempter, while warring against God, used humans as instruments for his nefarious purposes. When dealing with the line in the Lord's Prayer "Lead us not into temptation," Luther foresaw that no person could be spared temptation, but he added the observation that no one can be harmed by merely experiencing an attack, as long as it is contrary to a person's will and as long as he or she would prefer to be rid of it.

There was danger, he thought, when they were tempted, that believers would be drowned in seductions, which came in diverse forms. Youth get tempted by the flesh, adults and the aged by the world, while the devil beguiled strong Christians of any age. The following lines read like autobiography: if I am "chaste, patient, kind, and firm in faith, the devil is likely at this very hour to send such an arrow into my heart that I can scarcely endure." When this happens, he wrote, there is no place to run except to where one in faith can seize the Father. Luther had been where he was sure others would be drawn and where his own torrents of uncertainty took him, to what he named the abyss.

His comment on the creed concluded with an affirmation of the church as a community, a congregation, to which one is brought in baptism and nurtured on the Word. Here was a decisive demolition of any notions that Luther wanted to see the believer in isolation from community, as an individualist entrepreneur, a virtuoso or hero of courage and faith. He linked life in community with the life of forgiveness and the hope of the resurrection on the Last Day.

From the first, many of those who cherished the catechism memorized and analyzed it as if with attention to molecule-of-ink by molecule-of-ink or regarded it as if it were a weighty black hole of Luther's cosmos. To change the picture to one of light: All his other studied and formal teachings, he thought, radiated from the core teaching of the forgiveness of sins, like rays from the sun. From that center he had to take on the surrounding world again.

For Martin Luther, living the faith meant both testing one's own and contesting that of others, usually that of leaders in the papal church. In the second half of the 1520s, however, he argued most notably with a fellow critic of that church, Erasmus, and then with two other sets of evangelical challengers, Anabaptists over infant baptism and Zwingli and his Swiss colleagues over the Lord's Supper.

The first of these three contests, defined as a debate over the freedom versus the bondage of the will, reveals less about Luther's view of that will than it does about the extremes to which he could go when speaking about God. After several years of sparring, Erasmus late in 1524 in a hurriedly written *Dialogue on Free Will* attacked. He brought rhetorical skill and philosophical finesse to the book-length record of their conflict, while Luther countered with some creative bluster and theological audacity in what became one of his classic writings. Erasmus, eyeing Luther's great appeal to the masses, compared himself to a fly taking on an elephant.

The Rotterdam scholar sensed in Luther's bold defense of certainty some covering over of personal uncertainties. He raised a stabbing question somewhat like the one father Hans had asked when he questioned Martin's vocation to monastic life. Erasmus posed this: Luther, you have been attacking the fifteen-century-old church at its foundation and core. What gives you the right to do this? Why do you think that your interpretation of the Bible is the only true and certain one? How can you alone be wise, smarter than the doctors and theologians and saints? Luther had asked himself this, he admitted, with his heart racing after he first denounced the pope, the bishops, and their brothels: "Are you alone wise? Shall all the rest have been in error, and for so long?" His inner voice kept asking: "Suppose *you* are in error, and have seduced so many others into error, to be damned in eternity?" Still later he confessed that he heard: "Shall you, an individual and insignificant man, dare such momentous undertakings? What if you are the sole sinner? If God permits so many great ones to err, might he not permit one individual to do so?"

While he persistently struggled with his own doubts, in his reply of 1525, *The Bondage of the Will*, he attacked Erasmus' way of dealing with both doubts and skepticism. He scorned Erasmus for saying that in the face of complex questions he would submit to the authority of the church, whether he comprehended the issue or not. Luther gasped: "How can a Christian believe what he does not grasp?" For him, grasping meant holding only to the Word as revealed in the Bible.

The authority issue aside, Erasmus zeroed in on his central point, arguing that in biblical revelation people had the freedom to choose or to refuse the grace of God. Were this not the case, it would be folly to point to God as the active agent of justice and mercy. The Creator who had made people in the divine image expected them to act responsibly when making choices and would reward them for doing so. To Luther this logical-sounding claim meant trying to peer into the inscrutable mind of God. It was irreverent inquisitiveness, he added, to rush into those things that are hidden, not to say superfluous, in matters of faith.

Erasmus defined free choice as a power of the human will by which a person can either apply himself to the things which lead to eternal salvation or can turn away from them. Luther charged that his antagonist therefore confused the freedom that belongs to human nature, which was bound, with the derived and true freedom that comes with divine grace. When Erasmus accused him of obstinate assertiveness, Luther took that charge as a compliment: "Take away assertions and you take away Christianity." While Erasmus characteristically praised the modesty of skepticism, Luther wrote that the Holy Spirit is no skeptic, nor need humans be in respect to the revealed things of God. What the Holy Spirit by grace writes on the human heart, he insisted, is more sure than human life and human experience.

Luther pressed on, his language about God at this point revealing how near the edge of an abyss he could walk.

While he did not often repeat the drastic claims in *The Bondage of the Will*, he never withdrew or contradicted them either. They went like this: Only faith grasped the revelation of God, and even in this appearance God remained hidden in two ways. God was first hidden *in* the revelation, masked in the human grammar of Scripture or preaching and in the material bread and wine of the Lord's Supper and the water of baptism. Instead of coming only in supreme power, this God thus came in extreme weakness, humility, and suffering. God defied descriptions, definitions, and measures: "Nothing is so small but God is still smaller, nothing so large but God is still larger."

As warrant for his drastic claims about the reality of what he called a naked God who worked beyond the range of human vision and speculation, Luther cited Isaiah 45:15: "Truly you are a hidden God." But now he added that the startling assertion that God hidden *in* revelation is also hidden *behind* or *beyond* revelation. He thought that Erasmus' God was too easy to fathom and too readily accessible to human reason and striving and thus could not properly be God. Some features of the naked God would always remain hidden. Luther's language was terse as he summarized sharply: "We have to argue one way about God or the will of God as preached, revealed, offered, and worshipped, and in another way about God as he is not preached, not revealed, not offered, not worshipped. To the extent, therefore, that God hides himself and wills to be unknown to us, it is no business of ours. For here the saying truly applies, 'Things above us are no business of ours.'"

When it seemed that Luther could not be more radical, he added: "God must therefore be left to himself in his own majesty, for in this regard we have nothing to do with him, nor has he willed that we should have anything to do with him." Some critics began to contend that if God is hidden *behind* or *beyond* the revelation, anything goes, and nothing in the universe is reliable, so serious theology is impossible. How to speak meaningfully of a God who may be holding back from us what we might need to know in order to have faith and live the Christian life? Luther was aware of these problems and addressed the positive side of revelation with an affirmation about faith in the naked God, revealed but still masked: "But we have something to do with him insofar as he is clothed and set forth in his Word, through which he offers himself to us." That was more than enough.

Did the human count for nothing? Was God the only agent in history? Luther heard Erasmus argue that God, Creator of free will in humans, would never harden a person's heart. Luther countered with two main examples, one a biblical text in which God *did* harden the heart of Pharaoh in Egypt and another in which God was the potter and humans were merely God's clay. The most shocking words in Luther's effort to let God be God were these: "God himself does evil through those who are evil" and "Free will in man is the realm of Satan."

These bursts, designed to provoke Erasmus, exaggerated what Luther ordinarily stated more cautiously. He seemed up to this point to be making a very good case for a very bad God. He agreed that it was utterly repugnant to common sense for preachers like him to praise the greatness of divine mercy, when God appeared to be unfair, brutal, unbearable, taking pleasure in the sins and torments of some unfortunate creatures. Luther confessed: "This repugnant thought has caused many distinguished people of all times to go to pieces. And who would not find it repugnant? More than once it hurled me down into the deepest abyss of despair and made me wish I had never been born—until I learned how salutary this despair is and how close it is to grace." How close it is to grace! The idea made little sense to Erasmus, who would have nothing to do with Luther's witness to God abscondite, naked, nude, bare, hidden, masked, dark, or occult, but it was central for Luther and those who shared his gospel.

The Bondage of the Will extended his dark and risky teaching in response to one of the specific theses by Erasmus. Both scholars affirmed one biblical text asserting that God did not will the death of a sinner, but they also could read in some others that on occasion God *did* will death and damnation. So Luther saw himself forced to argue that a mysterious and inscrutable divine will lay behind whatever was revealed in the Scripture. This approach seemed to violate Luther's own principle that a person had to rely on clear words of Scripture for all basic teaching and belief. What could be more basic than the question of being saved, of being favored by God, or about the character of God?

Luther relied on and stressed scriptural assertions that witnessed to the freedom of God as he circled back to his grand personal question: "What is more miserable than insecurity?" He thought that Erasmus, speaking as if Scripture were unclear, would lead humans to another abyss, that of utter uncertainty. Instead, wrote Luther, the believer takes a leap of faith in a loving God, the God who appears in humility in the suffering and cross of Jesus Christ. "God hidden in his majesty neither deplores nor takes away death, but works life, death, and all in all. For there he has not bound himself by his Word, but has kept himself free over all things." *The Bondage of the Will* became a raucous hymn to the freedom of God.

Though the two contenders kept skirmishing after the publications of 1524 and 1525, the breach between them was final and complete. Luther in a taunt asked why Erasmus was so timid in the face of spiritual turmoil as the world neared its end: "To wish to silence these tumults is nothing else than to wish to hinder the Word of God and to take it out of the way. For the Word of God, wherever it comes, comes to change and renew the world." He added: "You do not see that these tumults and dangers increase through the world according to the operations of God. And therefore you fear that the heavens may fall about our ears." The once uncertain Luther now boasted: "But I by the grace of God see these things clearly, because I see other tumults greater than these which will arise in ages to come, in comparison with which these appear but as the whispering of a breath of air, and the murmuring of a gentle brook." With that statement, unsettling as it sounded, Luther found confidence. His will was in bondage, but in faith he said he found himself free, graced for other pursuits beyond that revealing debate.

. . .

The other two controversies of 1524–25 left the emerging evangelical movements divided and in disarray, in both cases because of disputes about the sacraments, conflicts whose outcomes left their leaders vulnerable in the face of papal and imperial threats. The two sacraments that evangelicals retained, baptism and the Lord's Supper, had not been mere rites, part of the decor of parish life, but the spiritual bedrock of life in Christendom. Rulers used the sacraments to determine who had a place in church and empire and who had not; those excluded could find the gateway to heaven closed. Evangelicals, over against such practices, had to determine what the two surviving sacraments meant in their own search for freedom.

Baptism was at issue after some Christians in and around Zürich refused to recognize infant baptism and insisted on "believers' baptism," the immersion of those who could testify that they had found faith. Their movements, called Anabaptist because they rebaptized adults who had been baptized as infants, spread rapidly, and looked ominous first to Zwingli and the Swiss and then to Luther, Melanchthon, and other Saxon leaders. The story of these more radical, sometimes pacifist but occasionally militant, movements is one full of persecution, of burnings and drownings, at the hands of established church authorities. It is a story that merits telling on its own, but here we shall have to restrict the narrative to Luther's response and the opportunity it gave him to spell out his defense of infant baptism.

The abrasion occurred because for the new movements of Anabaptists the benefits of baptism depended on faith, and in their definition infants simply could not have faith. In Luther's reading, proponents of believers' baptism had it exactly turned around. In his view, baptism occurred first, and because God initiated everything, faith came with it. In faith and through daily repentance, recipients of the grace associated with baptism grew in their appropriation of its meanings and received benefits lifelong. This did not mean that the baptized were to be exempt from subsequent struggle with doubt and guilt. Baptism might even intensify their inner conflicts, since in faith the baptized became especially attractive targets for the menacing devil.

Luther had to say that if the claims of Anabaptists were correct, then the church, which in his eyes had done something right through fifteen centuries of infant baptizing, had never existed at all. No baptism? No faith. No faith? No church. Even the mildest Anabaptists fought against such ideas as this one of Luther, and most of them were anything but mild when they defended themselves against his charge that their practices defied the command and denied the promises of God.

In January 1528 a law of the Holy Roman Empire, declaring believers' baptism to be subversive, stipulated the death penalty for Anabaptists, and authorities reinforced their resolve to pursue them after the Diet of Speyer a year later. Zwingli concurred in the penalty of death by drowning of some rebaptizers at their stronghold in Zürich. Luther first opposed the death penalty for Anabaptists in Saxony, following what he spelled out in 1525: Faith has to be free, and no one dare use coercion or compulsion to force conscience. Eventually Melanchthon and his own conscience convinced him that radical Anabaptists could be guilty of blasphemy and thus might be put to death by civil authorities. The less seditious among them need only be exiled, to end their threat to civil order. Some years later in the city of Münster, as it turned out, there were Anabaptists who did topple authorities. They set up communes and engaged in some violence, but most were soon thwarted, and numbers of Münster radicals in repentance or in backlash even returned to the Roman obedience.

At some stages of the controversy it is harder to tell what bothered Luther more: Anabaptism itself or the wildfire and chaotic way in which the movements spread, especially where its leaders did not insist on a called and ordained ministry. As for infant baptism itself, Luther had made his case long before the crisis, using a sequence of rationales. For a while he connected it with the biblical concept of a covenant, on the model of circumcision for Jews. Later he halfheartedly suggested that it was the faith of parents, godparents, and the worshiping community who presented the child for baptism that expressed faith for the infant. Since in his teaching, each person must believe for himself or herself, that approach was weak. Next he tried to show that infants believed, in the ordinary sense of the word, but he did not convince even himself of that. No, he decided, their faith had to be of an extraordinary sort. He also argued that no one could prove that Christians in ages past had ever withheld baptism from children. God would not have permitted a practice to prevail for so long were it false. That claim was troubling because he was simultaneously fighting against many traditional practices such as priestly celibacy.

One may ask, given these falterings, why Luther made so much of the practice. In fact, for his argument, the word *infant* mattered less than the word *baptism*, but it took the involvement of infants to make his main point, one he could never surrender. The Anabaptist view suggested that the believer brought something, namely the achievement of faith, to the act. He asked whether those who thought they had to bring faith to the symbol of baptism could ever be sure that they brought enough to be made right with God? If faith had to be in place before baptism and since people could not be sure of the extent and depth of their faith, how could they ever rest assured with God?

The only way to make clear the reality that a loving and covenanting God did all the saving work was to see baptism as nothing but a gift, a sign of God's initiative, an effecting of faith in the life of the infant. Beyond all the casuistry one thing was clear: Luther gave as the first reason to baptize everyone the fact that Christ commanded it. He quoted the call of Jesus to make disciples of all nations, *baptizing them*, and then continued by citing the end of the Gospel of Mark, where he heard Jesus say that those who believed and were baptized would be saved. Luther connected baptism with the promise of God, reinforcing this with words from the First Letter of Peter: "Baptism now saves you."

Let the Anabaptists rail; he thought that nothing other than baptism exemplified so well what he called a joyful exchange: The believer receives Christ's benefits as Christ takes on the condition of the sinner, whereupon the sinner gets declared righteous. It is almost as if for Luther, in some contexts, baptism equals justification. His *Small Catechism* of 1529 later gave succinct and precise form to his teaching. Baptismal water did nothing by itself but—no surprise—"the Word of God, which is with and alongside the water, and faith, which trusts this Word of God in the water," makes it "a grace-filled water of life" and a "bath of the new birth of the Holy Spirit." Baptism both signified and did something that happened *daily:* "The old creature in us with all sins and evil desires is to be drowned and die through daily contrition and repentance." As a consequence, "daily a new person is to come forth and rise up to live before God in righteousness and purity forever." Luther spoke of his experience of grace as his being born again; those who agreed with him now could speak of themselves as the daily "born-again" believers.

His *Large Catechism* urged a practice that could sound like a boast. When any believer needed strength and comfort, he should affirm, "I am baptized!" and go on to reason, "If I have been baptized, I have the promise that I shall be saved and have eternal life, both in soul and body." Luther connected the baptismal triumph with the struggles over doubt, a theme that pervaded his teaching and proclamation.

While the Anabaptist threat to church order and the practice of infant baptism remained, eliciting comment from Luther frequently also after 1525, he had to face another immediate sacramental issue, this time over the Lord's Supper. If disorder in the church provoked Luther to defend infant baptism, the problem of order in the political sphere demanded that he address the Lord's Supper. Politics indeed colored this conflict, which climaxed in a colloquy at Marburg Castle in 1529. Landgrave Philip of Hesse convoked it after hostile princes united against him and other evangelicals that year at the Diet of Speyer. He needed an alliance of newly named "Protestant" leaders associated with Luther in Saxony in one camp and with Zwingli in Switzerland in the other. Up to sixty princes, professors, and theologians who acted as seconds to those two main duelers responded to Philip's call.

The two antagonists there should have gotten along. Influenced by Paul, Augustine, and Erasmus, both were biblical scholars, ordained priests who became married pastors, leaders of evangelical movements, on the outs with Rome, and especially critical of the Mass. Both found constituencies among central Europeans who were chafing under papal and imperial strictures and who regarded the two as liberators. Despite their many parallels and agreements, however, they often crossed paths and at Marburg they figuratively crossed swords, especially over the Lord's Supper.

During their pamphlet warfare before Marburg, Zwingli, though less intemperate than Luther, could also rise to invective heights. He once called Luther's view of the Lord's Supper cannibalism, because Luther held that the bread and wine ingested by communicants *are* the body and blood of Christ. Luther in response sounded partly autobiographical, for he wrote during a bout of *Anfechtung* as he posed: "For what is certain in this life? Today we stand; tomorrow we fall. Today one has the true faith; tomorrow he falls into error. Today one hopes, tomorrow he despairs." Zwingli, he charged, was departing from the true faith, falling into error, and robbing believers of certainty. Such pamphlet warfare was a luxury in the academy, but for Philip an alliance was a necessity. Zwingli came eagerly to Marburg, with some hope of conciliation. Luther came mainly to please Philip but defiantly opposed Zwingli and offered no hope for agreement.

Luther argued on the basis of his dramatic formula that *the finite*—in this case, the bread and wine of the Lord's Supper—*was capable of bearing the infinite*, the resurrected body of Christ. Zwingli contended for the opposite. *The finite is not capable of bearing the infinite*, so the bread and wine on the table could not present, they could only represent, the resurrected body of Christ, which was now in heaven. The Lord's Supper for him was a memorial and symbolic event, to which worshipers brought their piety and good intentions.

The doctrine of Christ turned out to be the real issue. Coincidentally, around this season of turmoil Luther penned his most famous hymn, "A Mighty Fortress Is Our God," a song that has a bearing on the controversy since it included a startling and illuminating title for Jesus. In it Luther called him the Lord Sabaoth, "The Lord of hosts," and followed this with: "and there is no other God." The divine and the human were completely conjoined in Jesus Christ, so if God could be present everywhere and anywhere at once, Christ

could be at the right hand of God in heaven *and* in the bread
and wine. Looking for a moment like a biblical literalist,
Luther chalked the New Testament phrase "This *is* my
body" on the conference table, covered it with a cloth, and at
the proper moment in a dramatic flourish whisked the cloth
away to expose the biblical quotation and to fight for the re-
alism of the single word *is*.

Luther inherited what he regarded as a biblical worldview, in which finite elements like bread and wine could, as it
were, be transparent to the infinite. Zwingli regarded that
outlook to be an obsolete and offensive inheritance from the
papal church. What mattered instead was the faith and piety
of those who observed the commemorative and symbolic
Lord's Supper. Luther asked, in that case, what happened to
the gospel and in what way was pure divine grace needed, if
humans had to bring something by way of pious intentions
and thus good works to the event?

The Marburg debate soon grew repetitious and wearying. Some listeners wanted to hurry home, fearing the English sweat, an epidemic that was threatening the area.
Reports about the conclusion of the colloquy were mixed. A
teary Zwingli affirmed a friendship, but Luther reverted to
form. Having little use for softness, he snapped that Zwingli
should pray to God that he would come to the correct understanding of it all. One of Zwingli's seconds, the notable
theologian Johann Oecolampadius, wished the same to Luther
and his supporters. Each party was called to evidence Christian love to the other, as far as the conscience of each would allow it.

While the two sides under pressure agreed on some articles of faith, they divided over the one that counted. Luther, who said to a supporter of Zwingli, "You have a different spirit," told the Zwinglians that "we are not of one mind" and, therefore, "we commend you to the judgment of God." A frustrated Philip had to return to the political and military scene without an evangelical alliance to back him. Zwingli went on to theological and military contests in Switzerland where, serving as a chaplain, he was killed at Kappel in 1531. Luther was certain that his Swiss counterpart left too much to human effort and piety and thus contributed to uncertainty among the seekers. He moved on to new tasks and debates with others, confident that his views of Christ's presence furthered the search for certainty in faith.

CHAPTER FOUR

The Heart Grown Cold, the Faith More Certain

1530–1546

BY THE STANDARDS OF HIS TIME, as Luther neared fifty he was an old man, and his pace slowed somewhat. During his last fifteen years he kept preaching while he taught at Wittenberg, where he became dean in 1535. He produced probing Bible commentaries and a surge of other publications, many of them ill humored. He even soured on his long-favored environs. While it was near his end, in 1545, that he wrote Katherine about wretched Wittenberg, "My heart has become cold, so that I do not like to be there anymore," he had shown signs of chilling in 1530. That year he announced that he would preach there no more. But, of course, he did.

His liberating words in the 1520s had drawn such an enthusiastic response that he could picture a future in which the evangelical message and way of life would spread almost contagiously against all human opposition. His town, with its university, churches, and company of scholars, should have been the display case where Christians saw faith made active in love. Yet now citizens who had shared Luther's hunger for grace and assurance took grace for granted. He began to carry his vision of decline far beyond Wittenberg through Saxony and the Holy Roman Empire to Christendom and the whole world, whose imminent end he expected.

Alert to contemporary economic affairs, he used his rhetorical scythe to cut across all social classes, including swings at thieving servants. He stepped up attacks begun years before against people who in his eyes wanted to be both good Christians and good people in commerce. Usurers, those who took interest when they loaned money, were serving the devil. While he denounced grain speculators as thieves and killers, he also struck out against many folkways. Friendly to dancing, he pronounced current fashions in dances and apparel lewd. He asked students who lived with prostitutes to leave Wittenberg. Signs of greed dispirited him, and he asked, "What are we preaching? It would be better if we would quit." A plague that afflicted Wittenberg became a metaphor for the moral and spiritual condition of the public: "It seems that everything is lost."

He walked out on a congregation during a service when worshipers refused to improve their bad singing. Still, chilled as his heart had become when he looked for effects of his own messages, he did not lose faith in the act of preaching itself. He told evangelicals to threaten hellfire to the proud and offer paradise to the pious: "In the pulpit one should bare one's breast and give the people milk to drink, for every day a new church is growing up, and it needs the rudiments." And this man of paradoxes could also write his wife: "I do not leave behind a sad face of our congregations: they flourish in pure and sound teaching, and they grow day by day through many excellent and sincere pastors."

Remaining pastoral, he identified with and showed empathy to faithful communicants who suffered *Anfechtungen* with him, but his hopes now focused on the end of life and the end of the world. Believers who lived by faith should pray after the manner of a phrase he used when writing to his wife: "Come, dear last day." He told Christ's people that they were already past judgment in many ways: "If our hearts could grasp the fact that we need not fear the Final Judgment, what joy they would find."

While Luther's heart had grown cold about the local scene, he could well have taken compensatory comfort and seen signs to cheer him in the spread of the evangelical cause beyond Saxony and into many parts of northern and east-central Europe. He at least ambiguously affirmed some partisans of the cause beyond Saxony and Thuringia, even if they were not in complete agreement with him. He sometimes worked to build coalitions and mend fences among evangelicals, and he could sound sympathetic on occasion. After the theologian Zwingli was killed in battle in 1531, Luther, who still often spoke of the theology of his Swiss counterpart with disdain and at one time was not sure Zwingli would be in heaven, expressed regret about his death, fearing, he said, that now the Swiss would not be saved.

At the same time, the widening of evangelical influence brought ambiguities and problems. The most telling concerns came from some in the company of Luther. One of the most revealing and plaguing issues concerned John Agricola, a kind of protégé, who read how Luther ruled out the divine law as an agent in salvation and then carried the idea over to the moral life. To the shock of many, including Luther, this innovator taught that Christians should not preach God's law *at all* to believers. Having been made just, they were simply beyond its reach. After it became clear that Luther was unable to silence or convince Agricola, the two engaged in open conflict beginning in 1538. Luther eventually broke off relations, seemingly proud of his ability to sow discord when it resulted from standing up for his truth.

Agricola, it turns out, had exposed a difficult issue in Luther's witness when he asked why people who were made just by faith should do good, be good, or obey the works of the law. Luther did have answers to such questions, but his reliance on the theme of grace and of faith made active in love was not easy to articulate, whereas Agricola's simple dismissal of the divine law was popular among a following over whose growth Luther agonized.

He continued to receive friendly overtures from notable theologians such as Martin Bucer, whose influence was strong in and around Strasbourg. For years Bucer had shuttled between the Wittenberg school and the Swiss who gathered around Zwingli, but he had difficulty persuading Luther to have full confidence in him and his theology. After six years during which he made strenuous efforts to produce a document of concord, Bucer and his colleagues came in May 1536 to meet with Luther at Eisenach and then at his home in Wittenberg. At first Luther was gruff and kept some distance, wary as he was of their views of the Lord's Supper.

They sounded somewhat Zwinglian to him, though they were not. Eventually he met with Bucer, and they had it out over details of a conciliatory document that Melanchthon prepared for them. The Lord's Supper was again at issue. After Luther questioned the sincerity of the visitors, a tearful Bucer was ready to make concessions and did so, but Luther in the end only grudgingly signed the Wittenberg Concord which they drafted. Bucer and his companions by now had grown sufficiently close to Luther that the followers of Zwingli felt snubbed and marginal. Luther did maintain cool relations with the Zwinglians, now led by Heinrich Bullinger, but clearly the two movements were going their separate ways.

Luther and his friends had numerous dealings with rulers and theologians in the north, meaning Denmark, Norway, Sweden, Finland, and even indirectly Iceland. Frederick of Holstein in Denmark, who opened the way for the evangelical preachers in 1527, established their version of Christianity two years later. When Christian III took the throne in 1533, he deposed the seven bishops and named their successors, who were not clerics, superintendents. John Bugenhagen, who crowned Christian in 1537, followed up with a church ordinance that Luther endorsed also for Norway and Iceland. Christian exported students, herring, and money to the Wittenberg leaders, who mentored the Danes in this time of church change. Few of these shifts in ecclesiastical contexts represented radical theological adjustments on the part of the bishops, pastors, and people. Some resulted from turmoil among rulers and others occurred in response to the witness of a few important scholars who commuted to Wittenberg.

King Gustavus Vasa I in Sweden accepted the Wittenberg message as early as 1531, though it must be said that by the end of the decade relations between the unreliably pro-evangelical king and the Wittenberg leaders became strained. He relied on theologians Laurentius Andreae and Olavus Petri, students of Luther, to establish evangelical churches in Sweden. Petri became the archbishop of Uppsala, where the evangelicals retained apostolic succession, based on a belief that there was continuity through the ages from one generation of bishops to another through a rite of the "laying on of hands." Here again, politics played its role, as Gustavus exploited the influence of Luther and the Wittenberg theologians to his own advantage. By 1539 Luther was also paying close attention to Finland, whose leading agent of change, Michael Agricola, had studied at Wittenberg. These moves were not highly dramatic or abrupt. Not until 1544 did Sweden ban believers from expressing obedience to Rome.

As with moves into the north, there were weaker efforts to link with partisans of the cause in the east, in Poland, Transylvania, Bohemia, Moravia, Austria, and Hungary. These did advance through the 1530s, especially as students from such locales also came to Wittenberg to study. Luther did not give as high a priority to pursuing ties as one would expect, partly because of the recurrent disagreements over the Lord's Supper that showed up in some of these encounters.

More consistently, he was putting his energies into saving Saxony before the imminent Day of Judgment.

What mattered more than the geographical spread of the voice and rule of the evangelicals was their constant conflict with Rome. The pope and the emperor, having made peace in 1529 with the king of France, were free to court rulers in the provinces of northern Italy. They used their mutual fear of the Turk and their hatred of the evangelicals to motivate some joint actions. They resolved to work in concert to put down the evangelical irritation once and for all. To do that, they needed to win over as many princes as they could and then threaten those who would not come home to Rome.

Thus while the evangelical sphere of influence was expanding, the acts of the papacy looked ever more chilling to those who sided with Luther. Charles V had interests of his own all along in the churchly controversy. Wishing to prevent what he saw to be further breeding of schisms and threats to Christendom, he kept pressing for the pope to call a council, a move that Luther himself had been advocating since 1518. The successive popes had simply replied with a no: no council.

Through it all, Luther evidenced some wan but diminishing hope that there could still be a church council in which he could represent the cause and have a hearing that might induce Rome to make some changes. The persistent idea of a general council of the church developed through some revealing episodes. Thus an exchange in a meeting with papal nuncio Pietro Paolo Vergerio in 1535, who was sent to Saxony by newly appointed Pope Paul III to discuss the possibility of a council, showed Luther stating his bold claim, even in an arrogant taunt: "I hold a general free and Christian council such as the pope proposes to be highly necessary. I personally desire it, not for our sake. By God's grace we have no need whatsoever for a council, for we already have the pure word of God and teachings which lead to salvation, as well as churches where the ceremonies are conducted in accordance with God's word. The council will be healthful for other, foreign nations to whom our teaching might thus be spread."

Vergerio, dumbfounded in the face of such self-assurance, addressed the man he called Martine: "What are you saying, my dear fellow? Look to it that you be not too conceited, for you are mortal, and can err. Do you think you are cleverer, wiser, more learned and holier than so many church councils and holy fathers—than so many men of great learning throughout the whole world, who also honestly confess themselves to be Christians?" Whether spoken by an inner voice or presented by a challenger, that kind of question always stung, but Luther, now an experienced wrestler, stood firm.

Nothing came of the meeting. Luther angered the nuncio by declaring that if a council decided against him he would pay no attention. Even the prospect of being burned, he said, would not lead him to question his teachings. He did say, however, that if a conclave were to meet at a proposed site, Mantua in Italy, he personally would be there holding his neck out. By means of the uncharacteristically showy garb he wore that day, plus his joshing and off-putting speech, Luther had intended to jolt the Venetian, and he succeeded.

Vergerio reported to Rome that while he thought a solitary Luther might come to a council, he knew that the coalescing princes would reject the pope's chosen locale and everything they knew about the agenda. As late as 1545 Luther stated that he might accept papal governance but on terms he had to know were futile: The pope would have to accept that sinners receive forgiveness not through church tradition and authority but through faith in the death and resurrection of Jesus. It was not credible to expect the pope to accept such terms, so the dream of a council kept dying.

A new period began as imperial, national, and papal politics and military affairs dominated the scene when Emperor Charles V in 1529 convoked a diet in the small city of Speyer. His announced purpose was to unite the princes against Turkish armies. When he converted the occasion into an effort to rally forces against the evangelical challengers, numbers of resisting princes issued a protestation. All they got out of their efforts was a new name: Protestant.

The princes who had united at Speyer in 1529 came together again early in 1531 in the small city of Smalcald to form a league for the purpose of defending their Protestant territories in the face of the newly aggressive Charles V. War was on the minds of these rulers when they met with Melanchthon and Luther at Castle Torgau. The distressed princes asked the theologians whether Christians dared ever engage in armed revolt against the emperor. Though earlier

Luther rejected any such revolt except in explicit defense of the gospel, now he softened a bit. Being aware of how he always tried to keep secular and religious authority distinct, the princely seculars got him to say that it was up to them, not church leaders, to determine when revolt might be legitimate. Trying to square his view with his earlier call to obey earthly authority, Luther determined that if the emperor was acting in support of the papal Antichrist he would be acting against the gospel and must be resisted.

In 1530, when he crowned Charles emperor, the pope added an order to exterminate the evangelical heretics. To continue to hold the empire's place among European powers, however, Charles did not need their deaths as much as he had to have the help of their protectors, those Protestant princes. It became strategically wise for him to convoke a diet, which he called for the city of Augsburg in 1530. He was aware of four kinds of pressures above all others: from the pope, who was given to intrigues of his own; from the vacillating but aggressive Francis I of France, who kept the papacy off balance for his own monarchical reasons; from the territorial princes who opposed him; and, shadowing all other activities, from the threatening Turks, the Muslims on the eastern front. Charles wrote his wife in 1531: "The Turkish menace has increased so much that I have even considered coming to an agreement with the Lutherans in order to prevent worse disaster."

When the emperor summoned the Protestant princes and the evangelical theologians to Augsburg it became clear that the uninvited Luther could not safely attend. His allies spirited him away to Castle Coburg, the nearest safe post, but still four days of travel from the diet. Conciliation-minded Melanchthon was left to speak for the evangelical parties. He did so with some enthusiasm and with more hope than was warranted for better relations among Christians. While away from the scene of power, Luther supported his colleague even though he thought the whole venture was futile. He wrote sarcastically to court chaplain Spalatin that a wonderful work was being tried at Augsburg, which was to unite the pope and Luther, though both knew that the other would never make a move. As younger theologian Veit Dietrich commuted between Augsburg and Coburg to keep Melanchthon and other drafters in touch with Luther, the sequestered leader made his stand clear: "I will not budge an inch."

The accounts of Luther's stay in Coburg provide an opportunity to view the older Luther's quiet and slowed circumstances. From this hiding place he issued notes and left other traces that tell much about the state of his soul. Among these are a letter he wrote to his son Hans and an even more tender one to Katherine after she sent him a picture of their daughter Magdalena. Meanwhile, as he had at the Wartburg Castle, he grew a beard for disguise. His physical debilities multiplying, he had reason to complain about some distorting eyeglasses and he agonized when an old affliction returned in the form of a buzzing in his ears that accompanied severe headaches. The old abscess on his leg festered as before. His throat was sore and his tooth ached.

As at the Wartburg Castle, he took advantage of the enforced leisure to signal how he appreciated nature as God's creation, commenting when nightingales sang outside the window or jackdaws flew above the path. He was on good terms with the soldiers who had to keep watch on the castle and also with custodians, stewards, and cooks. On his walls he chalked two texts, one of them from his favorite, Psalm 118, that helped him affirm: "I shall not die, but I shall live, and recount the deeds of the Lord."

Relations between father Hans and son Martin preoccupied Luther when the hazards kept him from visiting his parent during his final illness. So the son wrote of his sorrow as he heard that his father's strong body was now failing him. He was sad because through the years some critics in the public had spoken and acted ill toward Hans because of Martin's ways. But, the son wrote, this abuse only confirmed the fact that the senior Luther was in the good graces of Christ. Martin wrote his father of his hope that the old man would not have to suffer much before the time came when others would flatten him out with a shovel. But the father would rise, he added with a bright triumphant note, as he assured the senior Luther that they would meet again in Christ's presence.

When his father died in April, Luther wrote Melanchthon that the death had plunged him into deep mourning, since he was thinking not only of the natural bonds but also of the precious love his father had for him. For through this father, he added, "God gave me 'all that I am and have.'" It was reassuring to him to know that his father fell asleep gently with a firm faith in Christ. His final testimony is worth quoting; yet "the pity of heart and the memory of the most loving dealings with him have shaken me in the innermost parts of my being, so that seldom, if ever, have I despised death as much as I do now."

Back at Augsburg, drawing on earlier documents, Melanchthon and his colleagues in four days patched together themes that they presented to an often dozing Charles. The relatively mild tenor of the Augsburg Confession, a feature that may have resulted from the fact that Luther was not its author, surprised many. It included no attacks on purgatory and indulgences, the Mass, or the papacy. Scripture and justification, the two themes most at issue, received very slight attention. There was no confessional article on the former, and the other, *Concerning Justification*, received only a half dozen lines. The drafters where they could underscored some points of congruence among the parties. Conservative about church order, they proposed that episcopacy might be allowed to survive if only bishops would teach the gospel and follow biblical patterns of oversight. A longish article, *Concerning Faith and Good Works*, was designed to show that the stress on faith did not detract from the fact that good works should and must be done, but of course, they insisted, this was never to earn grace, but for God's sake and to God's praise.

At the signing of this definitive document, few if any ordinary members of congregations, representatives of the priesthood of all believers on most levels of society, were present. The evangelicals stressed their ties to their princes. The Latin version of the text began with an epigraph, a line from Psalm 119: "I will also speak of your decrees before kings, and shall not be put to shame." Standing in for biblical kings, it turned out, were seven princes who signed the Confession. By excluding four others who favored Zwingli, however, they thinned their ranks. When the more assertive evangelicals got to read the document, some thought Melanchthon had been too compromising, too eager to keep the door open for restoring unity with Rome. Luther, though perhaps with not much enthusiasm, continued to support his colleague.

The emperor, recognizing the futility of pressing further, recessed the conclave and demanded that the Protestants return to the scene in mid-April of 1531. He also ordered his theologians to draft a Confutation of the Augsburg Confession, which they did. Eighteen of the evangelical positions that they isolated elicited no conflict, but both sides refused to budge on the others, which were those that mattered. Charles, still hoping for an acceptable document, insisted on one more draft. It was clear, however, that for him and his theologians some themes were nonnegotiable: The papal church was infallible; it would not change the understanding of the Mass as a sacrifice, would have nothing to do with the priesthood of all believers, must keep on insisting on celibacy for priests, and would still deny the cup to the laity at the Mass.

Melanchthon, who had looked forward to Augsburg as

the last moment in which jeopardized Western Christendom might come back together, now saw his hopes finally dashed. In his sequel, *Apology for the Augsburg Confession*, he looked back fondly but with regret and then into the future with concern. Now there existed a Church of the Augsburg Confession, which before long even Luther found himself calling "evangelical or Lutheran." Melanchthon and his colleagues had to make decisions about polity. The *Apology* said that this communion had wished "to retain the order of the Church and the various ranks in the Church," including episcopacy, even though its author had to emphasize that these had been established by human authority. The ancient fathers developed the episcopal form, he averred, for a good and useful purpose. But now the cruel bishops as its custodians were unfaithful to the gospel. In matters of faith and order, the breach was wide. When the pope finally called for a council that convened at Trent in 1545, it was simply and emphatically anti-Protestant.

For all his power, the pope did not have anything approaching complete control of the affairs that concerned him in the papal states around Rome. For instance, with the powers of the continent astir, Luther's old nemesis in England, Henry VIII, gave new troubles to the pope, who was sadly observing the progressive disintegration of Christendom. The issue was Henry's marital situation. Emperor Charles V had a personal stake in Henry's complex bedding adventures. His aunt Catherine of Aragon had proven incapable of providing a male heir to the throne for her husband. Thereupon the king contrived a rationale for an annulment and called for bargaining help from unexpected sites, including Wittenberg. In mid-1531 he asked theologian Robert Barnes, who was temporarily at the university there, to probe whether Luther might be of help in the circumstance. Melanchthon was ready to counsel a divorce, but Luther resisted that solution. He would settle for anything—bigamy, concubinage, or other arrangements—rather than support divorce. The biblical case against such a solution, he thought, was too strong for him to go along with Henry's desires. This stance dashed dreams for a churchly bridging of the English Channel and further developing of any ties between the monarchy and the Wittenberg school.

By the end of the year the strategic focus turned again to the territories in the Holy Roman Empire. The leaders of the Smalcaldic League consulted Melanchthon and Luther to see whether compromises might lessen tensions. The evangelicals showed some readiness to meet Rome halfway, since they had a sense of what was vital and what was less so. For one example, as at Augsburg some evangelical leaders were ready to see bishops restored among them, if only they would follow the gospel. Nothing came of that concession. Luther, one suspects with good reason, responded to the inquiries and appeals on many issues with the luxury of knowing that the Roman and imperial powers would not consent to even compromised offers. Still, he said he would cooperate in efforts to find churchly peace.

As prince after prince ignored or opposed proposals when these were in any way uncongenial, Luther came to sound isolated and insulted. Their actions contributed further to the chilling of his heart. He was disappointed that when he would give advice they would not follow, but if he withheld advice he suffered conscience pangs. When on occasion he intervened to please a prince and tried to help keep strong the strategic alliances against the pope and the Turk, he revealed his ineptness while he disappointed if he did not shock his partisans.

The most dramatic case in point was that of Philip of Hesse. An important leader in the Smalcaldic League and one who advanced Luther's cause, he was a womanizer who had been tied through an early arranged marriage to Christina, the daughter of Luther's political arch-foe Duke George of Saxony. Philip complained that Christina was surly and given to drunkenness—and she stank. He must have overcome the offensive odor enough to get close and sire the ten children she bore, three of them after he had taken a second wife without divorcing Christina.

While recovering from a bout of syphilis in 1539, Philip fell in love with Margaret von der Sale. Her mother insisted that Margaret could not be the prince's mistress; she would have to be his wife. Philip came to Luther to find a way through this mess, clothing his request in a slightly veiled threat. If the Wittenberg folks would not support him, for example by permitting divorce or bigamy, he might go to the emperor to get out of a bad marriage and into a better one. He also asked whether he could not in good conscience imitate the biblical patriarchs who, evidently with God's approval, had married more wives than one. No, said Luther,

God worked differently in the beginning than now. Nor could Luther sanction divorce unless there was evidence of adultery or a desertion which Philip's spouse would not forgive. A relative of the prince then urged Philip not to go whoring but to discipline himself the way the hard-drinking Prince John Frederick and other rulers did; that is, by choosing to lavish his affections and work out his desires on just one mistress.

Luther judged that taking a second wife was the least worst option, especially since Christina did not protest. She took pains to retain her rights and those of their children and to limit Philip when it came to the rights of anticipated children—there turned out to be seven—born of his second marriage. Luther meanwhile counseled the prince to commit the crime of bigamy and then lie about it. Philip took the advice and two months after the wedding sent a figurative card of thanks to Luther in the form of a barrel of wine. He could show gratitude, but he could not keep the scandal secret. Duke Henry fumed and other enemies used the news to discredit and oppose both Prince Philip and Doctor Luther.

Cornered and exposed, Luther rationalized weakly that his bad advice had been a confidential confessional counsel that issued from the law of love. A counselor, he explained, sometimes had to offer ambiguous advice that went against a norm in order to protect the norm, in this case that of marriage without divorce. That defense became incredible when the public learned that the unsatisfied Philip was still having extramarital affairs.

Melanchthon had dutifully drafted the illegal recommendation that Luther presented to Philip and had been present at the wedding. Now he experienced so much guilt that he became physically ill. Luther made a pastoral call on his friend, whom he hardly recognized in his traumatized condition. He lofted an angry prayer and addressed Melanchthon with a burst: "You will not die." He *dared* not die, since surrendering his spirit would be equivalent to committing suicide and that would only please the devil.

Melanchthon in due course did recover. Luther reported this to Kate, in a letter that suggested an unease barely disguised behind its mix of bravado and ease: "To my dearly beloved Katie, Mrs Doctor Luther, etc., to the lady at the new pig market: Personal. Grace and peace. Dear Maid Katie, Gracious Lady of Zöllsdorf (and whatever other names Your Grace has). I wish humbly to inform Your Grace that I am doing well here. I eat like a Bohemian and drink like a German; thanks be to God for this. Amen. The reason for this is that Master Philip truly had been dead, and really, like Lazarus, has risen from death. God, the dear father, listens to our prayers. This we see and touch, yet we still do not believe it. No one should say Amen to such disgraceful unbelief of ours."

Luther might have posed and chortled thus in private, but public attackers continued to give him reason to shrink in disgrace. He criticized a pamphleteer who, in support of Philip of Hesse, declared that bigamy was ethically neutral. No, wrote Luther: "Anyone who follows this fellow and his book and takes more than one wife, and thinks that this is right, the devil will prepare for him a bath in the depths of hell." Yet Luther, evidently voting himself out of hell, still maintained that a pastoral confessor in secret might have reasons to commend the lesser of two evils for the person he counseled. That counsel cost him dearly in reputation.

His secure role at the university gave Luther a base for work in the years when he said his heart was cold. Through it all, beginning in 1534 he began to publish biblical commentaries and, after 1539, his collected works. He claimed not to be eager to publish most of these, fearing that their appearance could distract readers from biblical texts themselves, but he used the occasion to give lessons to scholars. In a preface on how to study theology he stressed that even *Anfechtungen* were beneficial because they vividly reinforced the character of God's Word. These dreadful temptations led people to move beyond mere study into applying Scripture in their daily lives. Demonic assaults he called right, true, sweet, lovely, mighty, comforting, and wise since these *Anfechtungen* from God's enemy helped produce people whom Luther thought could be called the real doctors of theology.

In the case of volatile personalities, disappointment, frustration, and a sense of lost power can lead to rage, and Luther vented plenty of it in his senior years. His anger was never so evident as in his late attacks on three enemies beyond the Protestant circle: the pope as Antichrist, the menacing Muslim or Turk, and the Jews, especially the rabbis.

Luther read all three of them into the plot of the impending end of the world.

In 1545, during a season when the emperor was making moves toward a church council and the pope was thwarting them, Luther sided momentarily with the emperor and published *Against the Roman Papacy, an Institution of the Devil*. In it he treated the pope as a figure foreseen as the Antichrist in the biblical Apocalypse. Artist Lucas Cranach produced obscene accompanying cartoons that were more gross than Luther's violent verbal attacks. In a couple of instances even Luther thought the artist had gone too far when he pictured the pope being born through anatomical processes that Luther said were dishonoring to the female sex. It goes almost without saying that caricaturists from the company of the Antichrist in Rome fired away with equally gross anti-Luther pictures.

Luther reviewed some of the history of the papacy. He announced that here for the last time he would state the case that this Antichrist was a threat to all, an omen of the imminent Last Day. The pope was now a master of blasphemy and idolatry, a killer of kings and inciter of murder, "a brothel-keeper above all brothel-keepers and all lewdness, including that which is not to be named." Luther's affirmations that he would respect the pope even that late in history, if only the pope followed the gospel, were hollow.

The second target of Luther's flailings, the Turk, could have turned out to be as dangerous to the cause as was the papal Antichrist. While hunted almost his whole adult life and caught in the cross fire of conflicts within Christendom, Luther now had to calculate that all of Christendom together might not survive. Another religion, Islam, which Luther called Mohammedanism or the Turk, was advancing. This phase of the centuries-old threat began when Sultan Suleiman I took power in 1520 for a reign that roughly coincided with that of Charles V. The newly aggressive Turk swept across and captured the Balkans. After the fall of Belgrade in 1521 this Muslim force moved against Hungary and Austria. Buda and Pest succumbed in 1527. If the Turk would conquer Vienna, the European powers had to ask, what force could keep Turk armies from moving on toward Rome? Equally vulnerable were the territories and churches of Saxony, Thuringia, and Switzerland where Luther and Zwingli were preaching their gospel.

In the eyes of those who cherished Christian Europe, the result of military defeats would mean the end in more ways than one. To Luther, the advance of the Turk was another sign that the final day of God's judgment was imminent. If the pope was the prophesied Antichrist, the Turk was an avenger also foreseen in the biblical Apocalypse. Since Luther deduced that it was the devil who was inspiring the Turk to engage in false teaching, he felt called to counterattack. But at the same time, in his eyes, God was working behind the scenes, using the Turk to punish Europe. When princes did summon armies to fight in defense of Christendom, Luther the citizen finally went along with their call, but his message as a church leader to the public was simple: Repent!

Curiously and accidentally, the Turk turned out also to

be an unwitting strategic ally of Luther, Zwingli, and also the more radical evangelical parties, especially in the east. Some hounding of dissenters did go on there after King Ferdinand I, the brother of Emperor Charles V, in 1521 took over rule of the traditional Hapsburg areas in eastern Europe. In 1523 he declared his intentions against Luther and Zwingli and in the next year revealed that he wanted to go after them. It was the presence of the Turk that gave some princes a few years in which to make the case for some measures of religious freedom and, of course, to protect Luther and his company.

When King Louis II of Hungary fell to the Turk in the battle at Mohács in 1527, it was Ferdinand who stepped up to provide defensive leadership, even as he was still trying to eliminate the evangelical upstarts and their followers by enforcing the strictures of the Edict of Worms. Once again, only fear of assault by the Turk kept him from efficiently hounding and executing the critics of Rome. He, the pope, the emperor, and other kings and princes still had to work to keep coalitions together. They dared not alienate Europeans who identified with Luther. A common saying, long repeated in Austria, held that "the Turk is the Lutherans' lucky star."

Had these events all occurred in the years when Luther was young and on the rise, we would picture him nearer center stage. Instead, he now was being used only whenever the princes found it advantageous to exploit his word and image. He was still too prominent, too strategically placed in the politics of empire, merely to sit on the sidelines of history and wait for its end. His support, however, frustrated some political and military leaders because he was unwilling to stir Christians *as* Christians into battle. Thus his consistent stand now kept him from the front lines of anti-Turk propaganda and policy.

No foreign policy expert, he focused instead on a domestic issue in his tract *Whether Soldiers, Too, Can Be Saved.* They could. When public concern decreased slightly as the Turk drew back, he made little comment, but when the Turk again invaded Hungary in 1527 he finally stirred himself and published *On War against the Turk.* In it he defended himself against charges that he had been too passive about the need to fight wars.

That little book also gave him an occasion to develop a favorite theme central to his view of politics and war. He emphatically rejected calls by church and political leaders to turn a defensive war against the Turks into a crusade. The use of military power, he argued, could not be an explicitly Christian venture. Political rulers, presumably Christian as they were, *were* free to fight in self-defense, but they could never do so even then in the name of the church and never as part of a holy war. Temporal or secular authorities held only temporal or secular authority. This did not imply that there was no religious meaning in the death of soldiers; those who died in a defensive war, he claimed, could be considered martyrs.

Originally Luther discouraged financial support for the emperor and his armies as they held off the Muslims. When military leaders in 1542 pleaded, he complied with repentant prayers and prayed as if in paradox: "God punish us graciously." He also obliged the elector by writing a liturgy and, within it, a hymn:

> Lord, keep us in Thy Word and work,
> Restrain the murderous Pope and Turk,
> Who fain would tear from off Thy throne
> Christ Jesus, Thy beloved son.

The next stanza was a prayer that Christ the Lord would defend Christendom, but Luther would never be content to write a political and military hymn and let it go at that. He converted the theme into a hopeful invocation:

> O Comforter of priceless worth.
> Send peace and unity on earth.
> Support us in our final strife
> And lead us out of death to life.

In 1544 the elector joined Luther in calling for the people to repent. Seeing no signs of repentance, the compliant Luther declared that he still would pray, but only because the authorities demanded it, not because his heart was in it. His real concern was not with the still distant Turk but with the corrupt and compromising Christians closest to home. But if a Christian died while serving the secular prince in a defensive war, he professed, he would be among the holy ones of the most high of whom the prophet Daniel had spoken.

Closest to home, he urged Wittenbergers to advance the

cause of defending their place by praying and repenting. While he preached against the teachings of the Turk he doubted that his sermons on the subject had much effect. He did, however, write another little book, *Army Sermon against the Turks*, in which he called for the clenched fist, by which he meant tax payments to support defense.

Since Luther was called to be a theologian, he felt a need to engage in some theological critiques of Muslims in writings that took the form of outbursts. The apocalyptic belief that the world would soon end and that Judgment Day was near helps explain—though of course it does not excuse—Luther's final explosions. While prophecies in Ezekiel, Daniel, and the Apocalypse pointed to a time that in his eye resembled his own, he refused to predict either the when or the how of the end and rejected efforts by others to do so. Like so many who through the centuries believed the end was near but then often acted as if it were not, Luther connected its imminent coming with the ways of the pope and the Turk: "The pope is the spirit of the antichrist, and the Turk is the flesh of the antichrist," he wrote. "The two help each other to strangle us, the latter with body and sword, the former with doctrine and spirit."

In 1542 he set out to learn more about the Islamic faith, against which he was now preparing a Christian defense. That year, when he first came across and read a badly paraphrased Latin version of the Qur'an, he calculated that nothing would expose the falsehood of Islam better than spreading translations of the book in several languages. His program was clear: "To honor Christ, to do good for Christians, to harm the Turks, to vex the devil, set this book free and don't withhold it." He did not target the individual Muslim to become a potential convert to Christian faith.

Finally, Luther attacked the Jews. His assault, not racial but religious—and, hence, more dangerous—is most nearly explicable in the light of Luther's complex of disappointments that turned to anger. That his verbal attacks were religious, not racial, is clear from the fact that all through his career he hoped that Jews, as descendants of the ancient people of God, would convert to Christ. Profound disappointment was prime in his mind; when they refused to convert he judged them to be evil. The anger flared when, needing a villain, he charged the rabbis with misinterpreting the Bible and keeping their fellow Jews from coming to see salvation in Jesus. So he struck out at them as enemies of the gospel. Some Jews turned to him with hope, and he also denied them, thus blighting what had been developing as a record in support of human freedom and conscience. This turning of his back and then striking out at Jews came with no good reason at all except for his Christ-centered interpretation of the Hebrew Scriptures.

To answer the question why any Jew or tolerant Christian might look to Luther with hope, one has to go back to 1523, when he at first demonstrated a promise of better relations in a somewhat mild tract, *That Jesus Christ Was Born a Jew*. Some critics had accused him of denying the Virgin Birth of Jesus after he quoted the Bible to the effect that Jesus was of the seed of Abraham. His enemies insisted that such a claim contradicted the belief in Mary's own virginal conception. Luther felt he must answer their charges, and in the process of defending himself he sounded mildly sympathetic to Jews.

In the face of anti-Judaism in the church of Rome he reminded readers that Christians and Jews shared a common ancestry. Christians, he insisted, came late to God's family as outsiders and in-laws. True, back when he lectured on the Psalms, he attacked Jews as he would anyone else who thought they could please God by relying on the good works performed when they obeyed the divine law. He hoped that since now there was an evangelical alternative to Roman legalism, Jews would find it attractive and would convert. Very few ever did.

That Jesus Christ Was Born a Jew, not a major work in the Luther canon, does throw fresh light on some of its author's developing notions and commitments. When he claimed that church leaders who opposed him were treating Jews also like dogs, he charged that they were giving those Jews good reason to resist conversion. Jews, he pointed out, at least focused on the Old Testament, while many of the critics in the papal church consistently neglected the Bible. When he gave Jews credit for discerning that the pope was rejecting Scripture, he thought that he and Jews should have been allies of sorts, at least in what they negated.

Nine editions of that early tract appeared almost at once in cities where not many Jews lived. A largely sequestered few, devoid of military power or territories to defend, they displayed no will to assault Luther, yet his verbal blasts against the rabbis matched those he uttered against the Turk who menaced Christendom and the papal Antichrist who would kill him.

In 1536 he began to link with some provokers of anti-Jewish moves in politics. Elector John Frederick, who had succeeded Elector John in 1532, in the manner of rulers of the Holy Roman Empire, issued a decree that would banish the Jews from Saxony. To defend themselves, they counted most on the notable Jewish humanist Josel von Rosheim of Alsace, a respected scholar and ambassador to whom European Jews turned whenever challenged. Now in danger, some also looked to Luther, no doubt thinking that the author of the old tract would be open to defending them.

Part of his rebuff came seven years later when he wrote a sixty thousand-word tract, *The Jews and Their Lies*. It routinely repeated some traditional Christian rumors: that Jews poisoned wells and made off with Christian children to extract blood from them for cooking and sacrifice. Peripheral critiques in that book and elsewhere reflected a few standard Gentile cultural themes such as that the Jews who charged interest were usurers. He also passed on some whispered claims that Jews ritually murdered children and profaned the host, the bread that in the Lord's Supper *was* Jesus. But these were unoriginal and by no means central to his polemics. Nor did he emphasize one familiar late-medieval Christian critique, in which Jews were seen as the murderers of Jesus. Luther less regularly blamed Jews than wretched Christians for the crucifixion. In hymns and sermons he taught that through sinning, "we," not "*they*," had nailed Jesus to the cross. Instead of defending the hoary and lethal charge that

Jews had wished Christ's blood to be on their children, he wanted fellow Christian congregants to examine themselves and repent for what, he said, was their guilt.

Instead at the very heart of Luther's attack on the Jews was the observation that the rabbis opposed the Christian reading of the Hebrew Scriptures as Christ-centered documents, while Luther read them from a Christian Trinitarian point of view. From his treatment of the Jacob story and elsewhere in his writings we have seen that the Old Testament was to him entirely a book about Christ, the Messiah who was to come, as prefigured in those Hebrew Scriptures. By rejecting that interpretation Jews, dishonoring Christ, were in his eye dishonoring their own flesh and blood and were committing the ultimate blasphemy.

In tracts of 1543 Luther kept elaborating on the theme that rabbis were calling the Virgin Mary a whore and Jesus a bastard. Such teachers, he thought, found inspiration in medieval writing, the Kabbalah, to argue that Mary was menstruating when she conceived Jesus. In turn and in rage Luther felt licensed to use degrading imagery: that rabbis made Jews kiss, gobble down, guzzle, and worship the shit they were teaching, along with the Judas' piss of their biblical interpretations. His apocalyptic vision fired his already out-of-control imagination. He was appointing himself and his princes God's avengers. Fearing chaos as always, Luther did not urge Christian citizens to take matters into their own hands against their Jewish neighbors. Instead and in character, he called on civil authorities to banish Jews. With the

Day of Judgment at hand, it was urgent to keep Wittenberg and the rest of Saxony and Thuringia ready by keeping them pure. If Luther still uttered any slight calls for toleration, he designed these to help buy time in the hope that some Jews might convert before the end.

While urging the people not to avenge themselves, he did want them to stir up their rulers and joined in the calls for these leaders to burn synagogues along with the books of rabbis and even their homes, lest rabbis would change venues and find other places to teach blasphemy. If Jews would not respond to mercy by using the time given them to convert, he declared that Christians must drive them out like mad dogs lest they be damned alongside Jews.

To her credit, Katherine was among those close to Luther who were offended by incitement of persecution. She stood up to him, quoting Scripture in Latin, to which he made feeble reply. Melanchthon sometimes had to hold his nose when he passed along some of Luther's final malodorous tracts to Philip of Hesse, but pass them on he did. Philip in turn and on his own enforced anti-Jewish measures as he set out to banish Jews. Some of the refugees fled to Luther's beloved Eisleben, a fact that irritated Luther to no end. In 1546 in his last sermon, "Warning at the End," not showing any sign of repentance or change, he urged Christians to forgive Jews if they converted and if they ceased their offenses against the Christians. If not, he wrote, then they should neither tolerate nor suffer them to remain in the territory.

The once uncertain monk in these kinds of cases had become so comfortable with his certitude that it took on the character of the very self-centered security, the intellectual and moral self-assurance, against which he always warned. It served as his license to threaten others. The apostle of Christian freedom was not here free of his own theological prejudices. The biblical scholar and spiritual struggler who preached that, like Jacob, he had prevailed over God and man, in this display showed that he had not conquered his own worst self.

Halfhearted defenders pointed out that Luther was not singling out Jews and that his attacks were not atypical, that he was but voicing anew some themes taken from centuries of anti-Jewish rhetoric and policy that were being renewed in his time. Thus, despite all his reputation for tolerance, Erasmus as early as 1516 was praising France as "the purest blossom of Christianity, since she alone was uninfested with heretics, Bohemian schismatics, with Jews and with half-Jewish marranos." Erasmus wrote that he could do away with the Old Testament, if that would help set Jews back, and he wanted the whole of Europe to be as free of Jews as was France. Judaism, in his words, was the most pernicious plague and bitterest foe of the teachings of Jesus.

Similarly, Johannes Eck, Luther's foremost debating foe, rejoiced when the blasphemous race of Jews was persecuted, and if he heard softness from Luther, he could blurt: "It is the devil who speaks through you Lutherans; he would like nothing better than to acquit the Jews of their murders." One could adduce any number of figures like Erasmus and

Eck, but to suggest that everyone else was guilty does not exonerate Luther so much as provide a framework for approaching him.

On the positive side, Luther made it easy for later writers to assess his views of what he found most important, thanks to the friendly elector John Frederick. In 1537 John asked Luther to write a last will and testament to help make the case for a general council of the church, which he hoped would meet at Mantua. With the help of colleagues and after some arguments among them, Luther produced the Smalcald Articles, explaining that he wanted to spread those articles through the public press in case, as he fully expected and hoped, he should die before a council could take place.

The church of the Augsburg Confession included this personal document along with Luther's catechisms in its defining statements. He sprang not a single surprise as he etched this summary of his teaching, since his whole mature life had focused on the one teaching labeled *justification*, which he called the sun, the day, the light of the church. This had to be the nonnegotiable teaching and the rallying point for his associates in any proposed council. The seal on this testament was brash: "Nothing in this article can be conceded or given up, even if heaven and earth or whatever is transitory passed away." The voice was militant: "On this article stands all that we teach and practice against the pope, the devil, and the world. Therefore we must be quite certain and have no doubt about it. Otherwise everything is lost, and the pope and the devil and whatever opposes us will gain victory and be proved right."

On that theme turned Luther's revolution. He penned this terse summary of his lifework in a world of revolutions signaled by Copernicus' *De Revolutionibus* and Vesalius' *De Humani Corporis Fabrica* and two decades after Machiavelli's *Il Principe* appeared. The lifework summarized in those three documents offered radical approaches by geniuses who specialized, in turn, with work on the heavenly bodies, the human body, and the modern body politic. Luther's specialized in matters of the soul and in the God who created the universe and everyone in it and was embodied in it. This revolution began with a backward look, since it addressed issues posed during debate in the Middle Ages and rooted in the fifteen-hundred-year-old New Testament. But it also turned out to be pointed ahead for the human future, since the Day of Judgment impended, and meanwhile it contributed to drastic change in the way many Christians conceived their relations to God.

For Luther everything in his last will and testament came down to the reality that Christ gave up his own certainty to the point of death and, in perfect obedience, did what sinners could not do on their own, namely offer himself to God to give them forgiveness and assurance. In the Smalcald Articles he had to connect this once more with the works of love: "If one has a gracious God, then everything is good. Furthermore, we also say that if good works do not follow, then faith is false and not true." From this faith issued love, something he liked to treat epigrammatically: "Sinners are lovely because they are loved; they are not loved because they are lovely."

As with the long struggle over faith versus works, so Luther dealt to the end with the apparent conflict between faith and reason. In his last sermon at Wittenberg in 1546, he still called reason the devil's whore if humans employed it to reach for God and then claimed on its basis to understand how God operates. When Luther called such reason beastly, the ground of evil, the opponent of God, stinking, a pagan beast, a lazy-ass which destroyed true doctrine and was anti-God, he gave opponents ammunition to attack and allies occasion to misunderstand him.

To isolate his words about unredeemed reason and work out a whole negative philosophy on the basis of it would lead to a misunderstanding of the Luther who celebrated reason as God's gift in his catechisms and throughout his writings. He chose lifelong to be a university person, a student, a scholar, a researcher, who spoke in praise of the classics and other literature often dismissed as pagan. He encouraged liberal education and saw reason to be a divine gift that enriched ordinary life, undergirded science, and informed human affairs. In such causes, even Aristotle could have an honored place. In and after the joyful exchange with Christ, reason, redeemed, offered vast possibilities. Luther had seen reason as the devil's whore only whenever sinners stood before God trying to make their own case, but then it also became a handmaiden of God for pursuing whatever was good in human learning, in arts and law and medicine. Reason, the endowment that separated humans from animals, was the source of power, virtue, knowledge, and glory.

Along with his theological last will and testament he found informal ways to stress the personal issues, when as Pastor Martin he left signatures in Bibles brought to him. He scribbled this in one, typically because it stressed his theme of certainty, citing Isaiah 40:8: "The Word of our God will stand forever." This meant that "it remains fast, it is certain, it does not yield, it does not waver, it does not decline, it does not err, it does not let itself be diminished. Now wherever this Word comes into someone's heart with true faith it also makes the heart firm, certain, and secure, so that it becomes unyielding, upright, and hard against all *Anfechtungen*, the devil, death, and whatever may come, that it confidently and proudly may despise and disdain anything that wishes to doubt, waver, grow angry, or become enraged, for it knows that God's Word cannot lie to it."

On John 8:51: "A person would be called a good apothecary, if he could give such medicine that not only would it conquer death, but that death would never appear again. And it is a miracle that a person must die, and yet not see death when he has God's Word in his heart and believes in it. This sort of strong medicine is God's Word, when held in faith, for it turns death into eternal life. Oh, if someone could believe this, how blessed would he be in this life as well!"

Luther took almost a decade after writing his testament to say farewell to life, but he had soured on much that once sustained him. The couple owned a farm that Katherine had purchased at nearby Zöllsdorf. Luther advised that she should sell it while he was still alive. They could use the income he was still receiving to put it into shape for selling. A revealing sign of their times appeared when he commented that she would not enjoy being in Wittenberg alone, since citizens would hound her. One could speculate that he thought or knew that she lacked friends, that some of her brusque and abrasive ways made her unpopular, or that she might suffer from those who had no use for him. He took one more dig at the Wittenberg that had given him the cold heart and taken away his desire to be there: "I shall keep on the move and would rather eat the bread of a beggar than torture and upset my old age and final days with the filth at Wittenberg which destroys my hard and faithful work."

When Chancellor Gregor Brück heard of Luther's restlessness, he counseled him not to follow up on his impulse to sell the property, given the current real estate market. That advice may have been Brück's way of commenting that Katherine had made a bad investment when she bought the farm. Aware of Luther's rage against low morals among citizens in Wittenberg, town leaders also bade Luther to remain, promising they would effect change. They gave him friendly welcomes when he did visit or stay for any length of time. Still, the old zest was gone, and he often went through the mere motions of citizen life.

Physical suffering was often intense, for instance during an attack of kidney stones that occurred right after he preached at Smalcald back on February 18, 1537, nine years to the day before he died. The doctors on hand summoned a specialist who made a diagnosis. He had never been a good patient or follower of dietary prescriptions, saying he would eat what he wanted and would die when God willed. But that day he had to swallow the doctor's cocktail concoction of garlic and horse manure, forced down with quarts of water. Since he was Luther, he also joked about the low-quality beer they used to encourage the stone to make its tortuous way down his inflamed urinary tract. Some red wine or a rough wagon ride must have jostled the stone to the point that he could finally urinate. An upbeat Luther sang, "Praise be to God the father of our Lord Jesus Christ, Father of mercy and all comfort," on the night in which this God let him pass water and, as he added, earthily: "Thus does joy make me measure this liquid, so vile to others and so precious to me."

Soon after, at an inn at Tambach on the way home, Luther became sentimental about the people he would leave behind, notably Kate, for, as he summarized, "she was happy with me for twelve years." He worried that devotion to the gospel would be forgotten. In a premature and cautionary gesture, John Bugenhagen confessed him and recorded a practical last will and testament. Luther even discussed an appropriate burial place. Then a measure of health returned. For nine more years his records often dwell on his battles with stones, poisoning, pain, jaundice, and a form of uremic poisoning that quite likely helped occasion some of his erratic behavior.

Despite his own experiences of doubt and depression, his published *Table Talk* found him counseling others who suffered more than he. In various letters he detailed his own way of fighting back against despair. During his confinement at Coburg he had written advice to his children's tutor, Jerome Weller: Never be alone. Act foolish and play. Drink a good deal. It would even be a good idea to commit a sin— but not a gross one.

And the sufferer needed company. In a later letter he wrote his friend Nicholas Hausmann: "Unless I cling to the words of someone else my own knowledge is not sufficient." The most ignorant servant girl could console him in his aloneness, even if he had been prepared by his acquaintance with Scripture to find means to counter doubt. In the *Table Talk* he again described a way of facing the worst: "I'd sooner seek out John my swineherd than be alone," and sometimes, he said, he might even seek out the company of the swine rather than be alone when in doubt: "I've had help from people who didn't have as much theology in their whole body as I do in one finger."

Meanwhile, he recommended several strategies to aid in the wrestling. One might go hunting, riding, banqueting, engaging in sex—anything that would lift the spirit. Music helped. So did the clenched fist of prayer. Even his model Paul the apostle, he admitted, was not exempt from the need to wrestle. Luther wrote concerning Paul to his friend Justus Jonas, "I don't think he believed as firmly as he talks. I cannot believe as firmly either, as I can talk and write about it." He also confessed that sometimes when attacked from within, he had to change the subject or leave it behind. He told a visitor that imagining the eternal wrath of God was agonizing. He would change the subject when it came to mind. "There was a time when I thought about it a lot. God help me never to think about it again, but only of Jesus Christ, in whom we see the mercy of the Father." Still, reflecting on the phrase "I am baptized!" better than anything else led the believer to counter doubt, dread, and *Anfechtungen*.

At the end of the decade of his disease and depression he kept preaching and was even dragooned into making a trip in an effort to settle a dispute between the two counts of Mansfield, the town where he had spent his earliest childhood years. Some of Luther's own family had property interests at stake in the conflict. So in December 1545 he set out for Eisleben, but had to turn back when his companion Melanchthon's illness flared up.

During the period of postponement before some new talks scheduled for January 25, 1546, began, he preached at Wittenberg, where he called the congregation many chastening names. Using a text from Romans, he also spoke of the life on earth as a hospital existence and called for faith in Christ as a promised cure. Then Luther, with his three sons going part of the way, went to Eisleben without Melanchthon, who stayed behind to back the venture with prayer. A letter to Katherine carried tones of the old jocularity with which he so often greeted her as he commented on the quality of beer at various stops and joked that he was not tempted by beautiful women en route, which evidently was a signal to her that he was too weak to be tempted by anything or anyone.

Then followed a sequence of sermons he preached on his way at Halle and finally at his birthplace, Eisleben. The city clerk provided convenient living quarters next door to St. Andrew's Church. In sermons there on four different days he contrasted the faiths of the Turk and the Jews with the ways of Christian simplicity and certainty. Admitting that though the church was nowhere perfect or pure, he thought its teaching could be. So, doing what he thought would best help fortify the church, he ordained two new pastors. Even as he was urging faithfulness he had to cut off abruptly one last sermon. There was more to say, he breathed, and sat down, saying he was too weak to continue.

Luther's assistant on the scene, Johann Aurifaber, took special note now of his master's verbal ramblings. The scholar who regarded himself an old man at sixty-three spent most of his remaining energies speaking of his assurance in the face of *Anfechtungen*. "A Christian is only certain about the devil when he believes that Christ is his wisdom, salvation, righteousness, and redemption." While he said that kind of thing from the time when he was first convinced that he had a fresh grasp of the gospel, now he spoke urgently.

Luther near the end like Luther near the beginning wrestled as Jacob had. He strove still "with God and man" in the face of unbelief and despair, doubt and anxiety, terror and solitude. All his adult life he had been figuratively at the brook Jabbok, struggling through the night. Yet in his depression and in the darkness he always remained convinced that like Jacob he could surely appeal to the divine promise and draw strength from it. Though it always sounded unorthodox if not blasphemous, he witnessed each time that he had wrestled God and prevailed. In the context that he described in comment on Genesis, *he had conquered God and man.*

In Saxony in 1546 Christians of note did not merely die; they were expected to die in a ceremonial context. Families and spiritual counselors hovered and listened for almost liturgical expressions of final words, affirmations of faith and comments on hope. If that practice was common, it was especially valued in the case of Luther, so much had his inner life of faith already projected itself against the larger screen of European history. From there it cast reflections on others who looked for ways to live and die.

The dying man in question filled the role properly as he began picturing for others what he thought was immediately ahead. He was ready to die at Eisleben, but death could also come if he went home. Someone heard from him, "If I go back home to Wittenberg, I'll lie down in a coffin and give the maggots a fat doctor to eat." Earlier he had declared that he had lived long and was eager for death, "so that this miserable body may return to its home in the ground and be consumed by worms."

His health had not improved, though he told his wife it had. He was not up to being present when documents of concord were finally ready for signing by the brother counts who finally found reason to affirm an agreement. Now he tried to reassure Katherine that he was well taken care of and that the beer and wine at Eisleben were good. When his wife commented that she had heard of fire danger in his candlelit room, he reassured her. "Free me from your worries. I have a caretaker who is better than you and all the angels; he lies in the cradle and rests on a virgin's bosom, and yet, nevertheless, he sits at the right hand of God, the almighty Father." Katherine should be at peace.

It would surprise few that Luther, perhaps acting on a premonition and writing as he spoke, summoned a reference to his humanist education when he scribbled on a preserved piece of paper two days before he died: "Nobody can understand Virgil in his *Bucolics*, unless he has been a shepherd for five years. Nobody can understand Virgil in his *Georgics*, unless he has been a plowman for five years. Nobody can understand Cicero in his *Epistles* unless he has lived for twenty-five years in a large commonwealth. Let no one think he has sufficiently grasped the Holy Scriptures, unless he has governed the churches for a hundred years with prophets like Elijah and Elisha, John the Baptist, Christ, and the apostles. Don't venture on this divine *Aeneid*, but rather bend low in reverence before its footprints! We are beggars! That is true. February 16, 1546."

Contemporaries wanted to assess whether beggar Luther's trust in God endured, since this was a matter of interest to those who followed and agreed with him. After dinner on the 17th, at which friends discussed whether they would recognize each other in heaven—Luther was sure they would—he went to pray at a window, but suffered another attack. His instinct to lunge at opponents survived in a penultimate lick that hovering friends heard. They should pray, he urged, for the Lord God and his promise, that all might be well with him, for the Council of Trent and the accursed pope were very angry with God.

Confidant Justus Jonas at the end joined local preacher Michael Coelius in attending to Luther with prayer and hot towels. Two physicians appeared. Count Albrecht of Mansfield, one of the two brothers reconciled by Luther that week, offered what was said to be ground unicorn horn to counter pains in Luther's chest. Albrecht's wife, Countess Anna, who was supposed to know her way around the world of medications, was of some help. Interrupting their ministrations, the dying man proved he could remain polemical even in his call for the ultimate prayer, a confession to the God of all comfort whom Luther had believed, loved, preached, confessed, and praised but, he said, whom the pope and all the godless reviled and blasphemed. As Jonas recorded his prayer, Luther quoted John 3:16 and Psalm 31:5 in Latin and prayed the prayer of ancient Simeon from the Christmas gospel: "Lord, now let your servant depart in peace." And he addressed God, "Yet I know as a certainty that I shall live with you eternally and that no one shall be able to pluck me out of your hands." *As a certainty.*

Responding to a question as to whether he was ready to die steadfast in Christ and in the teaching he had long preached, he answered "yes" and fell silent. Countess Anna stepped forward with aqua vitae and rose vinegar to massage him. An enema did not help revive him.

Luther had had no opportunity to say farewell to Katherine or the children. Pastors and professors carried word to the widow, who expressed regret that she could not have been with him at the end. When Melanchthon, ever the academic, notified the Wittenberg students of the death, he commented that Luther, who had spent his whole career in the university, had been called to the heavenly university. Luther's burial in the Castle Church at Wittenberg attracted ordinary people, authorities, and nobles alike. Presiding Pastor Bugenhagen pointed out that Luther's grave was under the very pulpit from which he had sometimes preached. Melanchthon spoke as well, admitting that it was not always easy to work with the complex Doctor Luther. Still, the eulogist said he had admired Luther in a Christian manner, better than the way Alcibiades admired his Socrates, adding, "Every time I think about him, he seems even greater to me."

Katherine had to flee Wittenberg during the Smalcaldic War of 1546–1547 and to move with the university to Torgau when the plague came in 1552. Five days before Christmas in 1555, after she suffered an accident and fell into a ditch filled with cold water, she died and was buried in Torgau.

After Martin's death, Katherine mourned in a letter to a relative: "For who would not be sad and afflicted at the loss of such a precious man as my dear lord was. He did great things not just for a city or a single land, but for the whole world." The widow said she could not communicate the pain that was in her heart, and could not eat or drink or sleep. At the end, she commented: "And if I had a principality or an empire and lost it, it would not have been as painful as it is now that the dear Lord God has taken from me this precious and beloved man, and not from me alone, but from the whole world."

Bugenhagen, in a letter, quoted a prince who represented affairs in that world: "Previously we had two great rulers whom we had to obey, Luther in the spiritual realm, and the emperor in the temporal one." Luther was gone, but Charles V lived on to enjoy a victory in the Smalcaldic War, an outcome that did not exterminate the evangelical movements. When the emperor captured his Saxon foe Elector John Frederick and imprisoned Philip of Hesse, he could savor triumph. So when in 1547 the troops of this most durable and successful secular enemy of Luther occupied Wittenberg during that war, he marched into the Castle Church where Luther was buried. Someone urged him to do what amounted to the ultimate disgrace for heretics: exhume the body and burn the remains. Charles instead was ready with the sneer one expects from a relieved victor: "I do not make war on dead men."

In the company of the emperor in the church was an officer from Spain who attacked and slashed the face of Luther in a painting by Lucas Cranach. It is not likely that the slasher was aware of the language in the papal bull that once named Luther a wild boar loose in the vineyard, but he echoed it when he shouted that even after Luther's death, "the beast rages on."

Afterword:
Luther in the New Millennium

ASSESSING THE CONTRIBUTION of figures like Martin Luther, who characteristically spoke in apparently contradictory terms and exemplified a way of life that regularly called forth the Latin word *simul*, "at the same time," to deal with its dialectics, prompts some attention to the ambiguities in his legacy.

His stormy inner life has attracted the attention of reductionist psychologists and social scientists who would explain his impulses in only psychosocial terms, but at the same time he has evoked curiosity among nontheists who include in their analysis the intensity of his life focused in God.

As much as any individual he broke the hold of a single religious system and polity and helped free others to make basic religious choices on the basis of informed consciences, yet at the same time he stressed obedience to authority so strenuously that many who followed chose or were forced to conform and submit to those above them.

Therefore, while his form of religious discourse broke boundaries set by elites, at the same time he was so deferential to many kinds of authority that his followers often spoke less critically and less prophetically than he.

He and his generation set precedents by rejecting celibacy and affirming marriage and sexual expression, but he at the same time still conceived of women as operating under a "low ceiling," more or less confined to the kitchen, and helped perpetuate a culture in which women remained subordinate to men.

He was a hero to common people, attractive to peasants, a scorner of the pride of princes and wary of their lethal powers, but at the same time he so feared and abhorred disorder and chaos that he gave license to those who put down even legitimate peasant revolts and dismissed their concerns.

Luther denounced emperors, criticized usurers, and scorned princes in their pride, yet at the same time he offered and identified with political and social polities that in many cases led those who followed him to be passive and compliant in the face of the powers.

He could not have made more clear that the state was to be ordered by law and the church by the gospel or promise of God; at the same time he depended and called upon civil authorities to enforce features of the church's life when people failed to live by the gospel to his satisfaction.

He offered and promoted a theological rationale for open engagement by believers with the secular order, yet at the same time he brought into play apocalyptic terms and ideas which in the minds of many called into question the validity of investing in that very order.

Luther the humanist promoted education for citizens from childhood through university years, celebrated the created order of nature as a gift of God, and enjoyed the arts, especially music, because of their potential for enhancing human good, yet at the same time his apocalyptic views—the world would end soon—made it easy for the pious who followed him to downgrade nature and demean reason.

Being "under the Word," devoted to the Bible and divining meanings on its basis as few before or since have done, and free-spirited in his interpretations, at the same time because of his high view of biblical authority he made it possible for people of scholastic outlook to invoke literalistic approaches to Scripture in his name.

Recognizing Jews as more devoted to the Bible than most church people of the Roman obedience, at the same time he read their Bible, his Old Testament, in Christian terms and viciously struck out at them when they refused to agree with his interpretation or to convert to Christianity.

While at first he spoke with strong disfavor and later with only mild assent to seeing his work consolidated in a church called "Lutheran," at the same time he took no strenuous effort to prevent that naming, and today 64 million people around the world bear this man's name in their church identification.

Emphatically he was catholic in the sense that he identified with the church of all ages and places, professing belief in "one, holy, Christian, and apostolic church" as a single Christian flock, but at the same time his polemical style and theological self-assurance led him to be a basic agent of that church's dispersal in the Western world.

Thus he and his movement seemed furthest from the Roman church, but at the same time he left ecumenical openings through which his heirs still walk, as they did on October 31, 1999, when official Roman Catholicism and leaders of most Lutheran churches of the world signed a Joint Declaration on the Doctrine of Justification, a long but not complete step toward healing breaches on the basic point at issue, as inherited from the sixteenth century.

As the epigraph on the dedication page quotes him, he said "sin boldly," and did; and for those reached by his interpretation of the Christian gospel, he taught them to believe and rejoice even more boldly, as he did.

Luther was a man of conservative outlook in respect to much church life, but also a person of radical expression who took extreme positions. Through the centuries since his time, many have chosen to seek a safe middle between the ambiguous and often contradictory options available to them in his legacy. Whether many can or will choose to share his boldness in the new millennium will help determine how his influence will find expression in the centuries ahead.

Acknowledgments

THIS BOOK would not have been written had not Viking Penguin executive editor Carolyn Carlson thought it would be a good idea to have "Martin Luther by Martin Marty" represented in the Penguin Lives series. Ever since she invited me to write, in November 2000, she has helped me shape and reshape the chapters, keep the general readership in mind, and assist with all the other things an author hopes a good editor would do. I thank her for her guidance and inspiration.

Among Luther scholars, historians of religion and theology, historians and theologians, the following made critical comments on earlier drafts of *Martin Luther*, and I profited greatly from these: Denis Janz, Mark Edwards (who served as regular consultant), Larry Greenfield, Kurt Hendel, Richard E. Koenig, Myron Marty, the late David McCrea, Jonathan Moore (my longtime research associate), Linda Lee Nelson, Mark Noll, William Russell, Edward Schroeder, John H. Tietjen, Erwin Weber, and John Witte. The conventional word of caution and reservation is in order: None of them are to be held responsible for the flaws in this biography.

Representing "the priesthood of all scholars," nonprofessionals in this field, but of the sort Luther would have favored, include Mildred and Gene Burger, Jim Foorman, David Heim, F. Dean Lueking (my constant dialogue partner), Paul Manz,

Harriet J. Marty (alert listener to and reader of these pages, who made helpful suggestions), Joel Marty, Micah Marty (my literary partner, mapmaker, and picture editor), Peter Marty, Ann Rehfeldt, and those participants in adult education at Ascension Lutheran Church, as led by Pastor Roger Timm and Vicar Paul Elbert, who made written comments: Don Forney, Shirley Jan, Libby Shotola, Beth Smart, and Jean Turnmire. I thank them all.

Among those teachers, colleagues, and friends who taught and teach me Luther (though they don't always know it) on master's, doctoral, and postdoctoral levels, but who did not see this manuscript, are John Dillenberger, Robert H. Fischer, Gerhard Forde, George Forell, Brian Gerrish, Robert Kolb, William H. Lazareth, Jaroslav J. Pelikan, Michael Root, Franklin Sherman, Susan Schreiner, and Timothy Wengert; I must also mention the late Richard R. Caemmerer, Timothy Lull, and Lewis W. Spitz. The usual word of caution and reservation is in order: None of them are to be held responsible for the flaws in this biography.

The epigraph is from "Luther," from W. H. Auden, *Collected Poems* (New York: Random House, 1976), p. 235; used by permission.

For the record, not needing acknowledgment but rounding out the book in this last paragraph just as it started in paragraph one: *The Life Millennium* (Life Books, 2000) was a typical provider of lists mentioned at the beginning of this book, in this case "of the 100 people who made the Millennium." Martin Luther ranked third, behind Thomas Edison (!) and Christopher Columbus and just ahead of Galileo Galilei, Leonardo da Vinci, and Isaac Newton. The editors of this folly said "Let the debates begin!" Let them continue.

For Further Reading

NECESSARILY ESCHEWING reference to the vast monographic and specialized literature in English, let me offer titles most of which are broad in scope. Inestimably valuable is the *55-Volume American Edition: Luther's Works on CD-ROM*, edited by Jaroslav Pelikan and Helmut T. Lehmann (Fortress and Concordia, 2001). Using its word-search capability will help readers locate the majority of references to Luther's writings in this biography. In most cases I have quoted from this edition, but some of the translations of short passages are taken from works listed in the paragraphs that follow. Samples of Luther's more important writings appear in Timothy F. Lull, ed., *Martin Luther: Basic Theological Writings* (Fortress, 1989), recommended for classroom and reading-circle use. An invaluable reference that provides the context of Reformation themes is *The Oxford Encyclopedia of the Reformation*, edited by Hans J. Hillerbrand (4 volumes, Oxford, 1996).

On late-medieval trends and the Renaissance and Reformation, I have found three sources especially valuable: Anthony Levi, *Renaissance and Reformation: The Intellectual Genesis* (Yale, 2002); the durable work by Lewis W. Spitz, *The Protestant Reformation 1517–1559* (Harper and Row, 1985); and, from among the social histories, the books of Steven E. Ozment, who is representative of those on whom I have most depended in recent years; see his most expansive work, *The Age of Reform, 1250–1550: An Intellectual and Religious History of Late Medieval and Reformation Europe* (Yale, 1980).

Two recent volumes that offer vastly different interpretations of Luther's life are "between" books that provoked creative controversy: Heiko A. Oberman, *Luther: Man between God and the Devil* (Yale, 1989), and Richard Marius, *Martin Luther: The Christian between God and Death* (Belknap, Harvard, 1999). But see also David C. Steinmetz, *Luther in Context* (Baker, 2002), for the theological setting, and Bernhard Lohse, *Martin Luther's Theology: Its Historical and Systematic Development* (Fortress, 1999), for the most respected current comprehensive treatment of Luther's themes.

Very few biographies are in print in English. The great achievement of the century past, without which no scholar ventures to comment, is the three-volume work by Martin Brecht: *Martin Luther: His Road to Reformation, 1483–1521; Martin Luther: Shaping and Defining the Reformation, 1521–1532;* and *Martin Luther: The Preservation of the Church, 1532–1546* (Fortress, 1985, 1990, 1993). For those who seek more brief treatments, see the classic and best-selling if now dated work by Roland Herbert Bainton, *Here I Stand: A Life of Martin Luther* (Abingdon, 1950; current paperback, Meridian, 1995), which remains in print and still beckons; James M. Kittelson, *Luther the Reformer: The Story of the Man and His Career* (Augsburg, 1986), faithfully reflects the author's Lutheran background, while the ecumenical viewpoint of a Roman Catholic priest gives color to the magnificently illustrated Peter Manns, *Martin Luther: An Illustrated Biography* (Crossroad, 1982). Illustrations from the motion picture *Luther* (2003) appear in a short book designed to accompany that film, but which can also stand on its own: James A. Nestingen, *Martin Luther: A Life* (Augsburg, 2003). I have derived insights on the issue of faith and doubt from H. G. Haile, *Luther: An Experiment in Biography* (Princeton, 1980). Marilyn J. Harran, *Luther on Conversion: The Early Years* (Cornell, 1983), by isolating Luther's critique of *securitas*, was helpful to me in defining a main theme of his life for this biography.

Penguin
LIVES